Why Praise

Alvin J. Summers

Copyright © 2008 by Alvin J. Summers

Why Praise
by Alvin J. Summers

Printed in the United States of America

ISBN 978-1-60647-328-3

All rights reserved solely by the author. The author guarantees all contents are original and do not infringe upon the legal rights of any other person or work. No part of this book may be reproduced in any form without the permission of the author. The views expressed in this book are not necessarily those of the publisher.

Unless otherwise indicated, Bible quotations are taken from The King James Version of the Bible.

www.xulonpress.com

Dedication

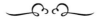

To a prayer that was heard,

A dream that came true

And a burden that was lifted,

God spoke, someone listened, I was blessed,

And now God will be glorified.

Contents

Forward By Dr. Russell Morrow ix
Acknowledgements.. xi
Preface... xiii
Introduction..xv
Chapters
  1. Glorify Me 17
  2. Trustworthiness...27
  3. Access 37
  4. Trusting in God 45
  5. I Declare War 53
  6. Being a Kingdom Carrier....................................63
  7. The Attitude of the Kingdom Carrier...................73
  8. King Jesus 81
  9. Absolute Devotion 89
  10. Being Holy and Being Human............................97
  11. Amazing Grace..109

Foreword
By Rev. Dr. Russell M. Morrow

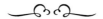

In this day and time when secular humanism, *(secular; the view that religious considerations should be excluded from civil affairs or public education; humanism an outlook or philosophy that advocates human rather than religious values)* is most prevalent in our society, where pop culture is setting the moral standards for our youth, corporate greed and governmental ineptness is hurting hard-working people and the church seemingly has lost some of its savor as the salt of the earth, The Reverend Alvin J. Summers raises a provocative question, "Why Praise?"

This question, "Why Praise?" speaks to the very issues that have put *"GOD- FEARING People"* in the predicament that we are in and offers us hope, deliverance and victory as he speaks with theological and practical wisdom rooted in the Word of God.

We live in a global community where news is instantaneous and much of the news is sorrowful and divisive showing us that the gates of hell are prevailing. As Christians, we have been commissioned by God to impact the world, our global community, for the sake of Christ. But the circumstances of life, all too often draws our attention from our mission and the deep things of God. Therefore, for many Christians their religion is cosmetic and their commitment is based on how things are going in their lives.

It is a fact that the world is a growing "Ball of Confusion" (To quote Motown's Temptations), but it is also a fact that God has been, and will always be, in charge when man thinks he's in control.

It is a fact that the world is a hostile environment for people who want to truly praise God with their whole heart, with integrity, with purpose in the kingdom of God, devoted, experiencing the grace and walking in holiness. But the good news is we can overcome the hostility of the world because of the love of God made known to us in the most practical ways through Jesus Christ.

"Why Praise?" reminds us, and rightfully so, that in spite of the fact we have sinned and walked in darkness in our past life, before our salvation, falling short of the glory God originally intended for us, we have been justified by faith in Jesus Christ to walk in the paths of righteousness ordered for each and every one of us in this hostile world.

"Why Praise?" tells us that even though we are challenged by God's Word to walk the straight and narrow instead of the proverbial wide road that leads one to destruction, the good news is that we can walk the narrow road with confidence and assurance. "Why Praise?" reminds us that God has empowered us through Jesus Christ to be victorious over-comers in our thoughts, word and deeds to the Glory of God.

I encourage you to prayerfully read this book with expectation, assurance and confidence. For in this book "Why Praise," God has a message of *Hope, Deliverance and Victory, just for you.!!!*

Acknowledgements

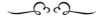

To the Oak Grove Missionary Baptist Church where I serve, thank you for 11 years of growth and experience. It indeed has been invaluable. To my wife Colleen and children, Cice and Autumn, who give of themselves while I do the work, thank you for the way that you love me. Without your understanding and compassion for what I do and what I am, my life would be so much more difficult. I am blessed beyond measure to have you sharing my life. To my Father and Mother, Nehemiah and Merdie Summers, who raised us in a Christian home so that we would have the tools necessary to repair ourselves as we traveled along the way. To my pastor Dr. May Field Brewster, God bless you for the example you set for us as we grew up. It has been and continues to be a source of direction and strength for my work in the ministry. To the late Reverend A.W. Terry and Dr. Lee R. Brown, I miss your wisdom, laughter, and fellowship. You have helped to shape my ministry in a way that keeps me practical as well as theological. Even now, I still hear you Rev. say," just love the people" and Dr. Brown as well saying, "I am the voice for the least of these." It is out of this context that I have found my way in moments of uncertainty and discomfort. I will forever be in the Lords debt for your blessing in my life alone. To Dr. David Boyle, thank you for your friendship and confidence in my ability

Why Praise

to be what God has ordained me to be. I continue to gain wisdom, leadership, and insight from your ministry and life. Also to Dr. Jimmy Latimer and the Central Church family who thought enough of what God had in me to bless my life with an education at Memphis Theological Seminary. I cannot begin to tell you the impact that experience had on my life. To all of those who sowed into this project to make it possible, words will never express my gratitude or appreciation for your gift of faith. To those who were subjected to being readers after the fact, thank you; Marcia Campbell, Kim Ware, Debra Boyd, Minister Chrys Hill, Natalie Boyd, Dr. Russell Marrow, Dr. Jessie Webb. Your insights were invaluable. And most of all I thank God for all that He is to me and those who believe in Him.

Preface

Are you tired of living a defeated Christian life? Are you sick of trying to overcome the same old things as if they are stronger than your God? Are you fed up with being less than you have the capacity to be? Well, I have good news. You don't have to be what you are, Christ died to make us free from the law of sin and death. There are so many believers that live beneath their privilege simply because they have not come into the knowledge of what Christ did at Calvary. We are free. They go to church week in and week out hoping for some hocus pocus action from the pulpit or in the praise service that will catapult them from one place to another. More often times than not they leave inspired but not motivated to attack their lives with Godly fervor for the sake of their condition as people of God. As a body we over work the preacher, the praise team, the musicians, the welcoming committee, the hospitality ministry and every other entity in the church simply because we are deficient in our spiritual development.

As believers, we are a promise manifested. God told Abraham that he was going to make him a great nation. So great in fact, that the stars would not be able to numerically hold the count. Through our belief in the Christ God made good on His promise. We are a promise manifested. It is from this position that you and I have to settle the matter

Why Praise

concerning whose we are, what we are and why we are here. Once we have settled those questions we must walk in confidence to live out their purpose in the earth. We may not be much to some but to God we are His handy work endowed with precious promises which allow us to escape the corruption of the world through lust because it is our Heavenly Father's good pleasure to give us the kingdom.

Introduction

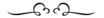

What does it mean to be an over comer when we live in a world of mishaps, schedules, tragic events and everyday afflictions. It seems that we are under attack in every phase of our lives. The enemy without and within seeks to invade our lives with sarcastic and cynical notions that undermine the saving work of Jesus Christ, so that as believers we seem to be less than we really are both to the world and to ourselves. We act defeated, look defeated, and walk defeated. We go to church out of ritual rather than expectancy. Which means, we go to church but we don't really expect much once we get there? We arrive with a "can't wait to leave mentality." Everything has to be time conscious fit to our schedule, so that we won't miss our next appointment. And often times, that appointment is nothing more than lunch after church or home to watch the game. The truth of the matter is that we have forgotten what it means to be more than conquerors through Him that loved us. We have gotten stuck in the routine of life and misplaced our victory over life. We live defeated because we are this worldly conscious. I am not suggesting that we should not be socially conscious, but I am suggesting that our social consciousness be driven by our position as children of God. Calvary was not a pretty sight. It was a painfully horrific ordeal but in the economy of God it was necessary to produce our liberation from

Why Praise

this present evil. Jesus endured many struggles so that we could have the posterity to say "I can do all things through Christ that strengthens me." He suffered with the intention to produce a people. That people produced by suffering ought not to forget their place in the world.

If you are in bondage, then you have believed the wrong story. Let me explain. One of the primary tactics of terrorist when trying to subdue a country or gain territory is to get the people they want to conquer to adopt a life of fear and submission. This is done through different mediums of torture at unexpected times in hopes of creating in them an acute awareness for safety. Safety becomes the driving force for silence, peace, and cooperation with the enemy. What the tactic is really seeking to do is engender a new story line within the tortured person so they forget what life was like prior to their enemy's intervention. So after a while it does not matter where they came from or what they were. Now they are prisoners of war. What the enemy has sought to do in the lives of believers through the malicious and vindictive acts of culture is to get us to forget what we were prior to his intervention. We were made in the image of God male and female. Humanity lived in a paradise filled with God's provision and His bounty. As his creation we wanted for nothing because it was our Father's good pleasure to supply all of our needs. Before the enemies arrival we were privy to the "Glory of God."

Chapter I Glorify Me

John 17:1
These words spake Jesus, and lifted up his eyes to heaven, and said, Father, the hour is come; glorify thy Son, that thy Son also may glorify thee:

Not long ago I posed a scenario to a couple of my choir students. I said, "What if I gave you 10,000 dollars to do with as you pleased?" The money is yours with no stipulations. What would you say to your friends if, or when they asked you where you got the money from? Would you say that you just had it or got the money on your own or would you say I gave it to you? One of them said I don't know and the other had no response. The jest of the scenario is whatever they decided to do with the money would have been fine because it was in their hands. The only snafu or hang up was they had to figure out where to put the credit for having gained the money in the first place. Have you ever observed children when they get a toy or something their excited about? Not the big kids but the small children. If you ask them who gave it to them they usually reply "so in so gave it to me" or point to the person if they can't talk. The freedom by which they give praise is a fascinating thing to watch because they are not plague with social issues of inadequacy or the need to be valuable. They just enjoy the privilege of life and living.

Jesus says in Matthew 18:3, except ye be converted, and become as little children, ye shall not enter into the kingdom of heaven. [4]Whosoever therefore shall humble himself as this little child, the same is greatest in the kingdom of heaven. It is out of this response that we come to the crooks of why we can't ask what we will. As a whole, we don't know where to throw the praise. In Acts 5 Peter deals with two people who chose in their heart to lie to the Holy Spirit. In that exchange he makes a statement in verse 4 that says, "Whiles it remained, was it not thine own? And after it was sold, was it not in thine own power? Why hast thou conceived this thing in thine heart? Thou hast not lied unto men, but unto God." The context of the statement that Peter makes gets at the heart of why we cannot be trusted with whatever we ask. It is because of what lies in our hearts. God not only looks at the actions of a person but the heart of a person. What we intend to do is as important sometimes as what we do. According to Romans 11:29, the gifts and calling of God are without repentance. In other words what God has given, God has given. It is in our power and we can do with it as we will. It is no secret God is good to all of us in ways we cannot even really express or comprehend. When we look at our lives God truly is in all things. I know at first hearing this seems to be a controversial statement but the truth of the matter is if God is not blessing us with it, He is giving us grace and mercy while we go through it. Why is God so good to us? Again according to Luke 12:32 it says, "Fear not, little flock; for it is your Father's good pleasure to give you the kingdom." In other words our Heavenly Father knows we have need of certain things to sustain life. It is out of this posture that He blesses us continually. Again, God is good. But is there another level of blessing we are privy to that we have not accessed because of that which lies in our hearts.

The text supporting the premise of this book comes out of John 17verse one. It reads.

> ❖ ¹ These words spake Jesus, and lifted up his eyes to heaven, and said, Father, the hour is come; glorify thy Son, that thy Son also may glorify thee:

1. Time of prayer

This text comes after dialogue with the disciples which set the framework for Jesus' hour of suffering in and for the world. Jesus lifted His eyes to heaven and began what I believe is necessary for any of us to start transformation. He prayed. Jesus realized the importance of prayer and meditation. Anytime a person is seeking to go to their next level or dimension in life prayer is an absolute must. As a general rule, it is all right to have friends and family but the ultimate voice of comfort and wisdom is God. Our relationship with God determines how we will experience life as a whole. But notice in this chapter that Jesus does not only pray for Himself but for all those connected to Him. This gives us an indication of how Jesus viewed relationships, praise, and success. Jesus Christ goes in prayer to set the stage for His next evolution and our elevation.

2. Sowing and reaping at the same time

Father, the hour is come; Jesus is saying the hour for which I was brought into this world is now. What was, is, and will be is contained in this moment. The eternal timeless perspective of God is being realized now. These words from the mouth of Jesus are setting in order the mindset necessary to carry Gods glory with integrity and confidence. Jesus understands His role in the Fathers redemptive plan for humanity and submits to the process. The law of reciprocity is set in motion but with one difference. By making the statement "the hour has come" the Lord is saying now is the time for sowing and reaping simultaneously. Anyone who understands the nature of farming recognizes you sow then you reap. There is a period of waiting for the harvest. Some of us have been sowing over the course of our lives waiting for the harvest to start. As a fellow believer, I want to admonish you to continue the sowing cycle because the harvest is inevitable. The harvest will come because it is the nature of the soil to bring forth harvest. And when we sow in God, we are guaranteed a harvest that will glorify God and bless our lives. So be not weary in well doing for in due season you shall reap if you faint not. But for Jesus, planting and reaping became one moment in time.

3. Glorify thy Son

Jesus made a command to His Father. He didn't ask Him. The command Jesus made to His Father rested in their relationship to and with each other. The purpose for Jesus' coming was to become the Christ the Savior of the world. Notice I said Jesus the Christ. Jesus was his name, but His sowing made Him the Christ. This moment was his hour to sow in pain and reap in joy. It was both a planting time and a harvest time. When Jesus says to the Father "Glorify thy Son" it was not a request but a command. This was not done out of arrogance, selfish agenda, or an acute need for power. The command of Jesus to the Father to glorify thy Son came out of Jesus trusting that the Father knew the heart of His Son. The fact that Jesus was willing to sow his life in the manner He did was proof enough of His commitment to Gods call and our condition. But when he says "that thy Son also may glorify thee" is a statement pending on the environment that beheld the action. In other words Jesus can sow His life, but whether or not he will get the harvest is up to the ones that behold or experience the event of Calvary because it is in our power to embrace the Christ or reject the Christ. If we reject His life, death, and resurrection we forfeit the power of the event to graft us in and cause continual harvest in our lives. If we embrace the event, then we become sons and daughters with the privilege to ask our Heavenly Father to glorify us, as well. And to glorify us is just another way of saying extol me or lift me that I may lift you. If you bless me I will not only give you glory but bring you glory. When they see me they will not only hear my praise, but they will see my praise. They won't just hear me say Hallelujah, but my walk will say Hallelujah. And there are a lot of people that give God praise, but they don't bring Him any praise. And that is what creates the controversy. The controversy is we sound like we are one of the righteous, a member of the holy and royal priesthood. But we act like one of them, the unrighteous. We preach prosperity and financial success but the question should be asked, "Why do we want to be rich, operate in a higher status, or live in a better place?" Our job as believers is to become trustworthy. In my estimation, it is not good logic to give somebody your belongings you can't trust. Most people would not give their money to a bank they thought was going to be robbed regularly. Why? The bank has not shown itself to be trustworthy. Why would God lodge in us the bounty of Heaven and Earth, if He can't trust us to do what we ought to with it? That could be one of the reasons why we haven't received our promotion and are still operating in the same place, because we can't be trusted.

Why would we want to say, "Father glorify me?" In essence the statement sounds kind of arrogant to say God glorify me. Given the rhetorical climate of the church at large, we are inundated with language the remind us of what we were rather than what we are. So then rather than Psalms 51:15-18 being an empowerment text it becomes a cage to keep us under control.

> ❖ **15**O Lord, open thou my lips; and my mouth shall shew forth thy praise. **16**For thou desirest not sacri-

fice else would I give it: thou delightest not in burnt offering. ¹⁷The sacrifices of God are a broken spirit: a broken and a contrite heart, O God, thou wilt not despise. ¹⁸Do good in thy good pleasure unto Zion: build thou the walls of Jerusalem.

In my opinion, often times, people use this text to keep people in bondage. Because they remind them of how filthy and wretched they are. They remind them of how broken they are. So people develop a false humility to keep down ridicule. It looks like we're humble but really in our heart we are still haughty. Most people have a misconception of what humility really is. Humility is not being a doormat. Humility is couched in the sensitivity to know that "Without God we could do nothing." It is broken. It is a contrite heart. It is a place where we give praise from.

Psalm 8:3 gives us definitive picture of our place in God and our inability to operate without Him.

❖ ³When I consider thy heavens, the work of thy fingers, the moon and the stars, which thou hast ordained; ⁴What is man, that thou art mindful of him? and the son of man, that thou visitest him? ⁵For thou hast made him a little lower than the angels, and hast crowned him with glory and honour. ⁶Thou madest him to have dominion over the works of thy hands; thou hast put all things under his feet:

This text reminds us we are somebody, but only because God said so. We have this saying, "put the devil under your feet." There are people who are trying to put things under their feet but are not connected to Him. There are other people who are trying to subdue enemies all to no avail. Our inability to subdue doesn't change the fact that we've been crowned with glory. But it does question what we are doing with our glory. It doesn't change the fact God has put all things under our feet. But the question still remains will those issues stay under our feet? It is our connection to the Father that provokes the stuff we are over to stay under. Because of ourselves, we have no real power. The only power we have is the power of who we are connected to. If we are operating off of our physical appearance, it will fade. If we are trying to contend through our mental prowess, we may develop Alzheimer's. We have to connect to something that will uphold us when everything else is failing.

Why we can say Father Glorify me

> Romans 8:14
> [14] For as many as are led by the Spirit of God, they are the sons of God. [15] For ye have not received the spirit of bondage again to fear; but ye have received the Spirit of adoption, whereby we cry, Abba, Father. [16] The Spirit itself beareth witness with our spirit, that we are the children of God: [17] And if children, then heirs; heirs of God, and joint-heirs with Christ; if so be that we suffer with *him*, that we may be also glorified together.

1. Notice how in verse 14 the text says as many as are led by the Spirit of God, they are the sons of God. This statement connects us to what I said earlier about the power of the event to produce a harvest in the lives of those who are affected by the event of Calvary or the life and death of Jesus who became the Christ. If we take seriously what happened at the cross then we no longer live in fear but in the spirit of family inclusion. We have been adopted through the act of Jesus and have the right to cry unto God as Pappa Father an endearing term that gets at the heart and nature of

our relationship to God the Father. So then we are no longer offspring by creation but children by blood. And if children, then heirs; heirs of God, and joint-heirs with Christ; if so be that we suffer with *him*, that we may be also glorified together.

2. Because we are family now with Jesus we have access to the family name and all that it represents.

Adonai-Jehovah — The Lord our Sovereign
El-Elyon — The Lord Most High
El-Olam — The Everlasting God
El-Shaddai — The God Who is Sufficient for the Needs of His People
Jehovah-Elohim — The Eternal Creator
Jehovah-Jireh — The Lord our Provider
Jehovah-Nissi — The Lord our Banner
Jehovah-Ropheka — The Lord our Healer
Jehovah-Shalom — The Lord our Peace
Jehovah-Tsidkenu — The Lord our Righteousness
Jehovah-Mekaddishkem — The Lord our Sanctifier
Jehovah-Sabaoth — The Lord of Hosts
Jehovah-Shammah — The Lord is Present
Jehovah-Rohi — The Lord our Shepherd
Jehovah-Hoseenu — The Lord our Maker
Jehovah-Eloheenu — The Lord our God

All of these identifiers of what God is capable of doing and being should give us courage to live out our purpose in the earth even though at times we are inadequate. Why would we ask God to glorify us? So we can bring God glory. And in God giving us glory, it is our hope that we will not mess up His name. We want our relationship to be based on a conviction and not how we feel at the time. Our ultimate aim should be to develop a disposition of trustworthiness in the sight of

God. As believers, we must learn to emulate the prayer Jesus prayed in the Garden of Gethsemane to aid in that process. Even though at times we don't feel like bearing life's cup, the Father put us in a position of trustworthiness. So we must learn to say, "not our will but Thy will be done."

Chapter II Trustworthiness

Have you ever gone through the day and asked yourself, "What just happened?" It's almost like the day was a blur of misfit moments. Nothing seems to go right and the more you tried to make sense of it all the more desperate and despondent you became. What you do for a living really doesn't bring you any satisfaction of intrinsic value. It's just something to do until something else comes along. In other words, we are just marking time. When we seek guidance from those around us, often times we get no real answers only fluff that leave us empty and more confused. But the key to tranquility and peace of mind is to find ones purpose for living. Pericles, a prominent and influential statesman, orator, and general of Athens during the city's Golden Age said, "What you leave behind is not what is engraved in stone monuments, but what is woven into the lives of others." People should remember who we are and what we did with our life. What they remember should impact them in such a way that it brings credibility to who we are as a people when we lived. In a world steeped with competitive moments and shallow philosophies it is apparent that we have reduced ourselves to what we have rather than who we could be. In an effort to be the best, we have desensitized ourselves from the necessity of caring about the people we are in relationship with as humanity. This creates in us an attitude of self

Why Praise

preservation at the expense of someone else's welfare. So then in the absence of real purpose, the pursuit of tangible assets becomes our goal for living. Only to find out that stuff, like people will betray us. We are driven to establish and maintain a level of life that keeps us satisfied and without want. Often times it is from this context that we seek and grope after God. We beg God for provision that will feed us until we want no more. Because God is a good God and is not willing to see us suffer want He supplies our needs. But what we have got to learn is that our Heavenly Father knows we have need of these things. Our problem is that we are two faced. We praise Him or throw Him the praise in places where it is convenient, but in other places where our witness could cost us provision we conveniently clam up and are silent. We praise Him not because He is God but for what He does. We don't lift Him because He is worthy, but because we have need of His bounty. We must decide what we want from God. Do we want Him or what He gives? Matt 6:24 says, "No man can serve two masters: for either he will hate the one, and love the other; or else he will hold to the one, and despise the other. Ye cannot serve God and mammon. ^{25}Therefore I say unto you, Take no thought for your life, what ye shall eat, or what ye shall drink; nor yet for your body, what ye shall put on. Is not the life more than meat, and the body than raiment? ^{26}Behold the fowls of the air: for they sow not, neither do they reap, nor gather into barns; yet your heavenly Father feedeth them. Are ye not much better than they? ^{27} **Which of you by taking thought can add one cubit unto his stature?** ^{28}And why take ye thought for raiment? Consider the lilies of the field, how they grow; they toil not, neither do they spin: ^{29}And yet I say unto you, That even Solomon in all his glory was not arrayed like one of these. ^{30} Wherefore, if God so clothe the grass of the field, which today is, and tomorrow is cast into the oven, *shall he* not much more *clothe* you, **O ye of little faith**? ^{31} Therefore take no thought, saying, What shall we eat? or, What shall we drink? or, Wherewithal shall we be clothed? [32] (For after all these things do the Gentiles seek:) for your heavenly Father knoweth that ye have need of all these things.

What we get out of these scriptures is an acute awareness of God for our condition as His creation. It is not the will of the Father that any should perish, but we perish for the lack of knowledge and a listening ear to the divine nature within. In order to have the desires of our hearts we must seek first the kingdom of God and its righteousness. These righteous pursuits become our purpose and without fail our provision. And though they tarry, wait for them for they shall surely come.

As a point of reference we are talking about, Why we can ask God to glorify us? Remember glory comes not for us alone, but for us to glorify. In other words, where will we throw the praise for the blessings given? Receiving God's Glory is about intention and not outward performance. We know how to sound like praise, look like praise, act like praise, but struggle with being a praise. Again I say, "We are two faced." An honest praise gets God attention. Our hearts must be for Him and not against Him. Listen at the indictment from Jesus in Mark 7:6: Well hath Esaias prophesied of you hypocrites, as it is written, This people honoureth me with *their* lips, but their heart is far from me. It is in the heart that God judges whether or not we are worthy of being glorified. This type of spiritual integrity or trustworthiness gets Gods' attention and releases our bounty.

When we are led by the Spirit of God or the Holy Ghost, we are God driven and God motivated. This means that God is acting through us to accomplish His purpose in the earth. This is why it is so important to be filled with the Holy Spirit or allow the Holy Spirit to have influence in us and on us. He is our connection to the attributes of God. At this point we are like our elder brother Jesus in the sense that we are doing the will of Him that sent us. In other words we are acting like obedient children and not ingrates. We are proving ourselves trustworthy.

❖ **My heart has been changed through my interaction with Jesus.**
2 Pet 1:2 Grace and peace be multiplied unto you through the knowledge of God, and of Jesus our Lord, ³ According as his divine power hath given unto us all things that *pertain* unto life and godliness, through the knowledge of him that hath called us to glory and virtue: ⁴ Whereby are given unto us exceeding great and precious promises: that by these ye might be partakers of the divine nature, having escaped <u>the corruption that is in the world through lust.</u>

Note that grace or favor and peace is multiplied unto us through the knowledge of God and of Jesus our Lord. The more we know about God the more we understand His favor for our lives and why Calvary was so necessary for our adoption process. Without Calvary we would not have any comprehension of Gods commitment to bringing us into His family. Calvary shows the lengths that He would go through to make us His own. As believers in the work of the cross, what we should want more than anything is to know Him so that favor and peace is multiplied in our lives. It is the favor of God that looks beyond our faults and gives us what we need. This confidence in the favor of God releases us from fear and ushers in peace that passes all understanding. We must as sons and daughters of God seek to probe the attitude and nature of God through His word and action in history, so that we can learn how to be worthy to receive His glory. In doing so we learn how not to act rashly or out of contempt, spite, or some other maladjusted emotion. We learn His thoughts, actions, and disposition concerning life and liberty. In other words, we learn how to make our Heavenly Father proud. His Son Jesus the Christ gave us a perfect example of how to follow. John 6:38 says:

- ❖ For I came down from heaven, not to do mine own will, but the will of him that sent me."

This knowledge of why Jesus came gives us a glimpse into what is necessary to ask God to glorify us. So then, the more we know about Jesus and what he would do the more we get a sense for what pleases our Heavenly Father. Provisions or the lack thereof keep us from serving with our whole heart. If we could just get to a point where we trusted God for our everyday bread then we could follow without fear of extinction. One of the things that caused animals to mutate throughout history was the environment around them. This innate quality kept and keeps them from completely being extinct unless their time is no more. As humanity presses in on their territory animals mutate, so they can survive. In other words, they go into survival mode. What has happened to us as believers is we go through transitions or environmental changes where we mutate to keep from dying or going without. So, we compromise our relationship to our Heavenly Father in order to meet our daily provision. We go into survival mode. But what we don't realize is that every time we compromise our faith for provision we are sending subliminal messages to our Heavenly that we cannot be trusted to be glorified. Listen at Luke 16 beginning with verse 10:

- ❖ He that is faithful in that which is least is faithful also in much: and he that is unjust in the least is unjust also in much. ^{11}If therefore ye have not been faithful in the unrighteous mammon, who will commit to your trust the true *riches*? ¹²And if ye have not been faithful in that which is another man's, who shall give you that which is your own? ¹³No servant can serve two masters: for either he will hate the one, and love the other; or else he will hold to the one, and despise the other. Ye cannot serve God and mammon.

Faithfulness is the key to our provision. We must have the assurance that our Heavenly Father knows that we have need of these things. Notice in the 2 Peter chapter 1 text that it never talks about wealth, money or daily provision not because it is not necessary but because it is implied. The divine power of God has given to us all things that pertain unto life and godliness. Most of the time all we focus on is the life and not the godliness. But it is the godlikeness that releases His glory on His sons and daughters. In other words God has given us everything we need to get His attention to release his glory, because life is more than food and clothing. He called us out of darkness into the marvelous light, so that we could be agents of His glory in the world. This was done in order that His kingdom could come on earth as it is in Heaven. Why give wealth and riches when the only one it would benefit is the one that it was given too. The whole use for wealth is to change the world with it.

> 2 Pet. 1:3-4
> ❖ ³ According as his divine power hath given unto us all things that *pertain* unto life and godliness, through the knowledge of him that hath called us to glory and virtue: ⁴ Whereby are given unto us exceeding great and precious promises: that by these ye might be partakers of the divine nature, having escaped <u>the corruption that is in the world through lust.</u>

The word virtue in the text carries with it a sense of eternal fidelity which comes in response to an interaction and empowering from God. Because of what God is to us and what God has done for us, and what God shared with us we ought to be forever loyal to the cause. Inherent in the word is this sense of what God is capable of doing through the yielded vessel. Our virtue or acceptability to God is based in Him forming us and making us what we should be. While the bulk of the responsibility for virtue lies in the work of the Father, virtue is also the attitude which the righteous must maintain in life and death.(G. Kittel, G. W. Bromiley & G. Friedrich, Ed., *Theological dictionary of the New Testament.* 1964-c1976. Vols. 5-9 edited by Gerhard Friedrich. Vol. 10 compiled by Ronald Pitkin (1:460). Grand Rapids, MI: Eerdmans.) Virtue is two sided. Virtue is both what God is doing in us and what we are doing because of our commitment to God. The transforming power of our virtue comes from a desire to please God with our fidelity or loyalty to His cause.

(The Woman with the issue of Blood) Luke 8:45
- And Jesus said, **Who touched me**? When all denied, Peter and they that were with him said, Master, the multitude throng thee and press *thee*, and sayest thou, Who touched me? [46] And Jesus said, **Somebody hath touched me: for I perceive that virtue is gone out of me.** [47] And when the woman saw that she was not hid, she came trembling, and falling down before him, she declared unto him before all the people for what cause she had touched him, and how she was healed immediately. [48] And he said unto her, **Daughter, be of good comfort: thy faith hath made thee whole; go in peace.**

Why Praise

Who touched me is the response of a person who was sensitive to the environment around them. It is not just a haphazard statement inquiring about a name, but a condition. The response of the disciples denotes their insensitivity to the condition of the people in the environment because they only sought the name of the person who touched Jesus. Jesus sought the condition of the person who touched Him. Jesus said somebody touched me for I perceive that virtue is gone out of me. The question should be asked, "Amid all of the people that were around Jesus accidentally touching Him, why was this woman the only one who provoked virtue to leave Him." I submit to you that it had to do with purpose. Jehovah Jireh, the Lord our provider's purpose for Jesus was the woman with the issue of blood. Those of us who have tried all else and are none the better for their efforts. Jesus came for folk just like that. Virtue left Jesus because of His commitment to His Fathers purpose. The life of Jesus was to establish that the Spirit of the Lord was upon Him. God had anointed Him to preach the gospel to the poor; Jehovah Jireh had sent Him to heal the brokenhearted, to preach deliverance to the captives, and recovering of sight to the blind, to set at liberty them that were bruised, To preach the acceptable year of the Lord. This woman got her breakthrough because her faith expected Jesus to know her condition and meet the need.

We are forever connected to God because of what Jesus did at Calvary. Our heir ship puts us in the family way. God calls us children. Out of this relationship, we come to know the magnitude of the great and precious promises of God. These precious promises become our provision for daily bread. As we come to know the Christ, we are infected by His nature and His attitude. We become partakers. This means that we are no longer just human but humans with an eternal resonance. Like the pebble or stone that is drop into the ocean deep and leaves ripples as it makes an impact is an example of how our lives should affect lives for years to come simply because we are partakers. We have a share in the divine nature of God. That is why the text says in 2 Corinthians 5:17 Therefore if any man *be* in Christ, *he is* a new creature: old things are passed away; behold, all things are become new. Through this relationship we have the ability to escape the corruption of the world through lust. Why? Because we trust the relationship we have with our Heavenly Father and believe He knows what we have need of. So then, the only real responsibility we have as children of God is to learn to trust in His provision and be trustworthy with what He gives us. We must strive to be a new creature.

Chapter III Access

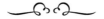

What does it mean to have all things under our feet? Or have access to all things of the sake of our existence as human beings? The hardest part about being human is the inconsistency of everyday living. But if we could get the concept in our minds that all things are given to us for the sake of our everyday living wouldn't life be a lot more bearable. To know that God Almighty takes a concerted interest in our seemingly mundane affairs is comforting to say the least. Have you ever had someone ask you how your day or week was going and genuinely meant it? Can you remember how comforting it was to know that they were not just playing niceties, but really cared about your welfare? Well magnify that by a gazillion and you have the love of God for all humans everywhere. God has taken upon Himself the responsibility of adopting us as His own through the unselfish righteous act of Calvary. To be a child of the living God is not just about heaven after while but life right now. It is the absolute assurance that God cares and is concerned about where we are and what we are going through. When we look at Jesus Christ and His generosity through suffering, we are engulfed by His willingness to be a sacrifice on behalf of His Fathers desire to save a fallen creation. The whole human race will forever be in the debt of Jesus for taking on the wrath of a jealous and holy God. As a matter of fact, He deserves the

Why Praise

title "King of Kings and Lord of Lords" which was and is to come forever and ever amen. Every knee should bow and every tongue should confess that there is no other name given unto heaven whereby people can be saved. Jesus deserves every accolade and promenade we can give because He is the access point and position for our deliverance from this place of wrath and tears. Jesus is the reason we can experience life more abundantly. He is the way the truth and the life. No person gets to the Father unless they pay homage and belief to the declaration of Calvary. It was there that we were grafted in and were made the righteousness of God. You, my brothers and sisters are somebody because God gave His son to make it so. At Calvary, Jesus proved His trustworthiness beyond a shadow of a doubt. The act of crucifixion took His life, but while suffering he looked through the corridors of history and said we were worth it all. His integrity was not found wanting. When tried by His everyday life, Jesus took it like the man of God He was and blessed humanity in spite of how he felt at the time. For even on that dreadful day Jesus was giving out invitations to paradise. Christ did the job of justifying us in the eyes of God and said to the one who sent Him and anyone who was listening "It is finished." Having said this, how dare we make the cross of none affect through our faithless response to work of Calvary. Life is filled with faith opportunities; Events that put our relationship and convictions to the test. There is a story in Mark Chapter nine beginning with verse 17 where a man comes to Jesus with His son who has what is said in scripture to be a dumb spirit. But through later inquiry, we find out that the spirit is demonic because it continually seeks to do the child harm. Jesus makes a very poignant and provocative statement to the father. Jesus said to him, if thou canst believe, all things *are* possible to him that believeth. The father in his honesty and extreme anxiety replies to Jesus' comment by crying out with tears in his eyes, "Lord, I believe; help thou mine unbelief." It is my opinion that we are in this same quandary today. We have needs, issues, tragedies and situations of the like that bombard us into believing that our Heavenly Father has forgotten that we are still here. It is almost as if we are saying as the disciples said on the ship in the midst of the storm "carest not that we perish?" But in response to our cries of desperation, Jesus is saying to us, if thou canst believe, all things *are* possible to them that believe. So then, the plight of the believer is to come into the full experience of what the demonic son's father said and reply, "Lord, I believe; help thou mine unbelief." But the question must be asked why do we struggle with unbelief? In most cases we are short sighted. If we don't get it now we lose faith that we will get it later. Second, we believe that we are more self sufficient than we really are. We have this idea that comes out of Greek philosophy that our worth comes from our mental or cognitive enlightenment and the attainment of possessions. In our minds, the more we know the greater we are. But the problem with that is that if enlightenment has no revelation or revealed truth on which to rely it is nothing more than philosophical jargon or at best good theories; everything that we are as human beings rest on the revelation of something else. Ultimately all revelation derives it advent from the benevolent heart of God. Through God's initiative He gave humanity an intellect and therefore we gain all reveled truth through that experience. Because God has released us to be all that we can be this ability to gain knowledge creates in us a sense of false pride that makes us believe that whatever we attain is from our own efforts and not His revelation. In order to become trustworthy in the economy of God, the believer must have a heightened sense of their unworthiness prior to the work of Christ at Calvary and an acute sense of dependence on Him after having accepted Him. In other words, if it had not been for Christ, where would I be? There is a saying in addiction circles that goes something like this, "except for the grace of God there go I." The implication is that no matter how blessed I am right now things could have been different. One of my favorite passages of scripture is Ps. 8 verse 3 because the writer recognizes their smallness in scheme of God's universe:

- ³When I consider thy heavens, the work of thy fingers, the moon and the stars, which thou hast ordained; ⁴ What is man, that thou art mindful of him? and the son of man, that thou visitest him? ⁵ For thou hast made him a little lower than the angels, and hast crowned him with glory and honour. ⁶ Thou madest him to have dominion over the works of thy hands; thou hast put all *things* under his feet: ⁷ All sheep and oxen, yea, and the beasts of the field; ⁸ The fowl of the air, and the fish of the sea, *and whatsoever* passeth through the paths of the seas. ⁹ O LORD our Lord, how excellent *is* thy name in all the earth!

As created beings we have this unworthy worthiness about us that humbles us and lifts us all at the same time. There is this independence of the world and this dependence on God. We are in the world, but not of this world. We are unworthy of the blessings that our Heavenly Father bestows, but worthy because He created us in His image with the responsibility of being overseers of the works of His hands. To be created in the image of God gives us priority as it relates to having provision. Because our heavenly Father knows that we have need of certain things in order to live, that is why he gave us dominion over the works of His hands. The problem that faces the believer is the task of becoming a good steward and remembering that God is the owner of that which we have charge over. While it may be in our hands it still belongs to our Heavenly Father. In the book of 2nd Chronicles chapter 16, we find the story of Asa's demise. In

Why Praise

---

chapter 14 however, we get an introduction the life of Asa. The text reads:

- ❖ So Abijah slept with his fathers, and they buried him in the city of David: and Asa his son reigned in his stead. In his days the land was quiet ten years. ² And Asa did *that which was* good and right in the eyes of the LORD his God: ³ For he took away the altars of the strange *gods*, and the high places, and brake down the images, and cut down the groves: ⁴ And commanded Judah to seek the LORD God of their fathers, and to do the law and the commandment.

In Chapter 15 we see the zeal of Asa for the cause of God magnified.

- ❖ ¹² And they entered into a covenant to seek the LORD God of their fathers with all their heart and with all their soul; ¹³ That whosoever would not seek the LORD God of Israel should be put to death, whether small or great, whether man or woman. ¹⁴ And they sware unto the LORD with a loud voice, and with shouting, and with trumpets, and with cornets. ¹⁵ And all Judah rejoiced at the oath: for they had sworn with all their heart, and sought him with their whole desire; and he was found of them: and the LORD gave them rest round about. ¹⁶ And also *concerning* Maachah the mother of Asa the king, he removed her from *being* queen, because she had made an idol in a grove: and Asa cut down her idol, and stamped *it*, and burnt *it* at the brook Kidron. ¹⁷ But the high places were not taken away out of Israel: nevertheless the heart of Asa was perfect all his days. ¹⁸ And he brought into the house of God the things that his father had dedicated, and that he himself had dedicated, silver, and gold, and vessels.

Notice that Asa was on fire for the things of God so much so that he took his own mother off of the throne because she had made an idol in a grove. Asa was a man of God with a conscious to do what was right. But when we get to chapter 16 we see a turn in his character. He starts to think for himself and stop depending on the care of the Father. This is where you and I have to be careful. And the text reads:

❖ ¹ In the six and thirtieth year of the reign of Asa Baasha king of Israel came up against Judah, and built Ramah, to the intent that he might let none go out or come in to Asa king of Judah. ² Then Asa brought out silver and gold out of the treasures of the house of the LORD and of the king's house, and sent to Benhadad king of Syria, that dwelt at Damascus, saying, ³ *There is* a league between me and thee, as *there was* between my father and thy father: behold, I have sent thee silver and gold; go, break thy league with Baasha king of Israel, that he may depart from me.

1. Fear forced him to make an alliance with Benhadad king of Syria that was not endorsed by God.
2. He took provision out of the house of God to secure the alliance.
3. The provision that he took was vowed to God by covenant agreement. In other words he took what was promised to God and gave it to something that was not endorsed by God.

❖ ⁷ And at that time Hanani the seer came to Asa king of Judah, and said unto him, Because thou hast relied on the king of Syria, and not relied on the LORD thy God, therefore is the host of the king of Syria escaped out of thine hand. ⁸ Were not the Ethiopians and the Lubims a huge host, with very many chariots and horsemen? yet, because thou didst rely on the LORD, he delivered them into thine hand. ⁹ For the eyes of the LORD run to and fro throughout the whole earth, to shew himself strong in the behalf of *them* whose heart *is* perfect toward him. Herein thou hast done foolishly: therefore from henceforth thou shalt have wars. ¹⁰ Then Asa was wroth with the seer, and put him in a prison house; for *he was* in a rage with him because of this *thing*. And Asa oppressed *some* of the people the same time. ¹¹ And, behold, the acts of Asa, first and last, lo, they *are* written in the book of the kings of Judah and Israel. ¹² And Asa in the thirty and ninth year of his reign was diseased in his feet, until his disease *was* exceeding *great*: yet in his disease he sought not to the LORD, but to the physicians.

Asa lost perspective on what mattered most. His life and provision were in the care of His Heavenly Father. Everything that he had need of God provided for the sake of their covenant relationship. When Asa focused on his situation and not his covenant relationship he essentially said to God I can protect this people through my own initiative and savvy. I don't need your approval or sanction. I am the King of Judah. Little did he realize that the people he made an alliance with, were going to fall subject to his command. They escaped because he focused on his provision and not his trust in his Heavenly Father. The text says he got so angry with God that he inflicted pain on others and would not call on God in his own sickness. Pride will make you do some stupid things. His healing and deliverance was in the relationship he had with God, but because of pride he died.

Chapter IV Trusting in God

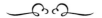

The first thing we have to get through our heads as believers is that all things are ours for consumption and usage. Everything that God made was good. It is here for us to enjoy and experience, but in the proper context. The trouble with us is that we don't know when enough is enough. We are chronic over users. It seems in every aspect of our lives we must be in constant watch of over doing our lives. We find one or two things that really excite us and we take on a tangent, to the neglect of something else. The key to a healthy and productive life is balance and moderation. Have you ever heard the saying that God knows just how much you can bear? All it is really saying is that God is a God of balance. Not too much sorrow and not too much happiness but plenty of joy. God gives us things/experiences that transcend our ability to understand or comprehend. That is why the bible says in Philippians 4:4 Rejoice in the Lord always: *and* again I say, Rejoice. It is in our redoing of joy that we get perspective on what we are going through and find purpose and meaning as we overcome. Overcoming is a process for us, but a promise from God. So then, what we are in process of doing as believers is developing a mindset to trust God in all things. Lord I believe, but help my unbelief is the negativity we are trying to eradicate from our vocabulary as children of God. We must learn to rest on the assurance that we are not forgotten nor forsaken because God said so in His Word. According to 2 Corinthians chapter 1 verse 20, "all the promises of God in him *are* yea, and in him Amen, unto the glory of God by us." That means every promise that God has made is true and relevant to our lives as believers. God wants to give us glory so that he may be glorified. In this process of glory people come to know the true and living God is not slack concerning His promises. We are meant to overcome in all things. Romans 8:31:

> ❖ [31]What shall we then say to these things? If God *be* for us, who *can be* against us? [32] He that spared not his own Son, but delivered him up for us all, how shall he not with him also freely give us all things? [33] Who shall lay anything to the charge of God's elect? It is God that justifieth. [34]Who *is* he that condemneth? *It is* Christ that died, yea rather, that is risen again, who is even at the right hand of God, who also maketh intercession for us. [35]Who shall separate us from the love of Christ? *shall* tribulation, or distress, or persecution, or famine, or nakedness, or peril, or sword? [36]As it is written, For thy sake we are killed all the day long; we are accounted as sheep for the slaughter. [37]Nay, in all these things we are more than conquerors through him that loved us. [38]For I am persuaded, that neither death, nor life, nor angels, nor principalities, nor powers, nor things present, nor things to come, [39]Nor height, nor depth, nor any other creature, shall be able to separate us from the love of God, which is in Christ Jesus our Lord.

We have got to get through our intellectual psyches that we are the children of God. We reason ourselves out of a breakthrough by second guessing our faith. If God *be* for us, who *can be* against us? As we look more deeply into the cited text we find that there is nothing that you and I will face that God has not already covered in His plan of provision for our lives. He fixed our sin problem in His son Jesus. He fixed the judgments and criticisms of people by making us His elect. He gave us purpose for life when He justified us as a viable entity in the creative process. He gave us an advocate that intercedes on behalf of our condition before Him in the event that His wrath would arise and consume us. What demonic spirit of adversity shall separate us from the love of God in Christ Jesus? No not one. As we train ourselves to trust Him we gain a confidence that we are over comers and that we shall not be moved. For what the devil means for bad God means for good. And every time God brings us through, we are left with another event that solidifies who and what God is to us. We don't know how He does it but it all works out for our good. God is a God of balance and purpose.

All things are ours and for our living. The key to all things continuing is to keep the relationship with God and His purpose at the fore front of every endeavor. Don't let anything or anyone keep you from being found trustworthy by God. Obstacles come to galvanize our commitment; because as believers, we have already been made victors over our circumstances. Often times what keeps us from being faithful or full of faith is what we see in front of us. We get discouraged, disheartened, and ultimately give up because we've forgotten that God is a God of balance and purpose. Whatever we are going through at that present time is programmed to pass over. Our Heavenly Father knows just how much we can bear. Our job in the process of life is to make good choices that echo the sentiment and direction of the Holy Spirit.

1 Cor. 3 beginning with verse 16:
- ❖ [16] Know ye not that ye are the temple of God, and *that* the Spirit of God dwelleth in you? [17] If any man defile

the temple of God, him shall God destroy; for the temple of God is holy, which *temple* ye are. [18] Let no man deceive himself. If any man among you seemeth to be wise in this world, let him become a fool, that he may be wise. [19] For the wisdom of this world is foolishness with God. For it is written, He taketh the wise in their own craftiness. [20] And again, The Lord knoweth the thoughts of the wise, that they are vain. [21] Therefore let no man glory in men. For all things are yours; [22] Whether Paul, or Apollos, or Cephas, or the world, or life, or death, or things present, or things to come; all are yours; [23] And ye are Christ's; and Christ *is* God's.

It is a wonderful thing to have people who can speak words of life into us, but God is the source of all knowledge and wisdom. If you are going to make it through the daily grind, you must have a leading of God for yourself. The Holy Spirit must be your voice of conscience. The church at Corinth was much like the church of today in that they had issues with who was most important. There were factions who aligned themselves with particular preachers to the neglect of their relationship to Christ. Some said I am with Paul others Apollos and still others Cephas, but no one said I am of and with Christ. Paul tells them the best place to be is with the Lord because all things are of Him and all things are yours because of Him. So, then every person has a right to the same provision as another. I am not more privileged as a pastor just possibly more faithfully obedient or do diligent. I am not telling you not to follow leadership because God has put leaders over us to guide and strengthen our lives. But as a believer, you have a right to access Christ for yourself. You are a promise manifested.

Romans 4:13 says:
- ❖ For the promise, that he should be the heir of the world, *was* not to Abraham, or to his seed, through the law, but through the righteousness of faith.

Galatians 3:6
- ❖ ⁶ Even as Abraham believed God, and it was accounted to him for righteousness. ⁷ Know ye therefore that they which are of faith, the same are the children of Abraham. ⁸ And the scripture, foreseeing that God would justify the heathen through faith, preached before the gospel unto Abraham, *saying*, In thee shall all nations be blessed. ⁹ So then they which be of faith are blessed with faithful Abraham.
- ❖ ¹⁴ That the blessing of Abraham might come on the Gentiles through Jesus Christ; that we might receive the promise of the Spirit through faith.

Zechariah 8:12
- ❖ For the seed *shall be* prosperous; the vine shall give her fruit, and the ground shall give her increase, and the heavens shall give their dew; and I will cause the remnant of this people to possess all these *things*. ¹³And it shall come to pass, *that* as ye were a curse among the heathen, O house of Judah, and house of Israel; so will I save you, and ye shall be a blessing: fear not, *but* let your hands be strong.

How do we come to believe that our heavenly Father will see and answer prayer both spoken and felt? We read, study, meditate on His precious promises and resolve that God will and cannot lie. Romans 4:13 say we have a promise that God would make us heirs through our faith; but heirs to what, prosperous or peaceful living. We are that remnant through faith. So, then our faith is what we must develop in order to

Why Praise

walk in abundant living. Remember, we are not walking in faith just so we can prosper, but so that our Heavenly Father can be glorified. We want blessings so that we can show off the goodness of God to the world. They need to know that we can be people of integrity, moral character, lovers of God and still be prosperous. We are defeated because we tarry too long in emotional places that remind us of what we left behind when we accepted Christ. When Christ did the ordeal of Calvary there is now no more condemnation to them that are in Christ Jesus who walk not after the flesh but after the Spirit. Life moves even if we don't. The only constant is change itself. So then, we must determine how we will move as life changes.

> Joshua 24:14
> Now therefore fear the LORD, and serve him in sincerity and in truth: and put away the gods which your fathers served on the other side of the flood, and in Egypt; and serve ye the LORD.
> [15] And if it seem evil unto you to serve the LORD, choose you this day whom ye will serve; whether the gods which your fathers served that *were* on the other side of the flood, or the gods of the Amorites, in whose land ye dwell: but as for me and my house, we will serve the LORD.

What do you need to leave behind? What is keeping you from serving Him in sincerity and truth? Is it connected to where you've been or who you were with? Today choose sides. There is only one reason why we won't leave Egypt. We have war in our members.

> Romans 7:21
> ❖ [21] I find then a law, that, when I would do good, evil is present with me. [22] For I delight in the law of God

after the inward man: ²³But I see another law in my members, warring against the law of my mind, and bringing me into captivity to the law of sin which is in my members.

Chapter V I Declare War

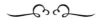

At some point in our relationship with God we must take a stand against anything that keeps us defeated and broken in our lives. We must get through our heads that we are more than the experience we have had or the things we have been through. While, they are a part of our lives they do not define us completely. We are somewhat of a complex being in that we have the ability to choose what will define us. So often times we allow the wrong people, places, and things power to characterize our lives. They hold us hostage for what they want from us. We go to different venues and see stuff that remind us of where we've been and what we've been through and it creates havoc in our spirit simply because we have given that situation more power than it deserves. Consequently, we live broken defeated lives because we didn't know when to say enough is enough. Today I commission you to say with me. **I declare war**. War against anything that would seek to make us less than God made us to be. I declare war against any obstacle that would block my path and hinder my progress with God. I declare war against a mindset that reminds me of where I've been rather than where I am going. I declare war against the enemy. What is our enemy? Anything that would keep us bound and stifles our freedom as children of God. From this day forward I charge you to be the people of God with victory in your heart and destiny in your eyes. But before we can move forward in our new declaration of freedom, we must put a sign up that says no fighting allowed. This ground is holy ground.

> 1 Cor. 6:19
> ❖ ¹⁹What? know ye not that your body is the temple of the Holy Ghost which is in you, which ye have of God, and ye are not your own? ²⁰For ye are bought with a price: therefore glorify God in your body, and in your spirit, which are God's.

You and I were bought and paid for through the actions of Christ at Calvary. We are no longer our own. We belong to God. Therefore, as stewards of God's property we declare there shall be no fighting here. We are the temple of the Holy Spirit. He lives and breaths in us. So, unless He endorses the fight, there will be no fighting or warring on God's property. This means that even if you have to subdue yourself for the sake of yourself, it must be done. And just as a point of clarification, never be so in love with where you are that you can't see that where you are may be wrong for where you are going. Never loose the skill of saying goodbye, even if it hurts when you leave.

> Romans 7:22-23
> ❖ ²²For I delight in the law of God after the inward man: ²³But I see another law in my members, warring against the law of my mind, and bringing me into captivity to the law of sin which is in my members.

The war that rages within us is a mindset that suggests the old man is still alive and breathing. It is tied to memories that won't die. The old person tries to speak to us and influence us from the grave. Notice that Paul uses a word in the text that suggests an intense battle as if dominion for territory was at stake. He says, "I see another law in my members warring." The literal meaning of the word in the original language is to make a military expedition, or take the field, against anyone to oppose, war against. So then, when Paul uses the word warring he is literally saying there is a fight going on in my members for control over my destiny. I know and love the law of God. I know it is good for my life, but my carnal nature won't let me move on without reminding me of what I'm giving up. Here are some points of interest as spoken by the Word of God.

Romans 8:6-10
- ❖ ⁶For to be carnally minded is death; but to be spiritually minded is life and peace. ⁷Because the carnal mind is enmity against God: for it is not subject to the law of God, neither indeed can be. ⁸So then they that are in the flesh cannot please God. ⁹But ye are not in the flesh, but in the Spirit, if so be that the Spirit of God dwell in you. Now if any man have not the Spirit of Christ, he is none of his. ¹⁰And if Christ be in you, the body is dead because of sin; but the Spirit is life because of righteousness.

The carnally minded person in the text is driven by a this worldly desire prone to sin because it does not have divine influence.

1. Carnally mindedness is death
2. Carnal mindedness is enmity or hatred against God
3. To be carnal means having the nature of flesh, under the control of the animal appetites which can not please God
4. Therefore we are prone to sin and oppose God.

But if we have been born again, the old nature has been crucified with Christ and I in the formal sense is gone, and I in Him, the Christ, is born. I am not a puppet on a string with no conscious reality of what is going on around me; but a human being who has submitted their will to the care of a Heavenly Father. As believers, we do what he says simply because we have come into the knowledge of Gods divine nature and the power of that nature to will grace and peace multiplied in our lives. When we trust and obey the will of the Spirit we say to God no more I but Christ. Not because we can't do something else, but because we don't want to do anything else. We give over our wills because Christ by example gave over His will for His Fathers purpose. As we deny ourselves and take up our cross daily, we give over our wills in hopes of pleasing our Father just like Jesus did. This act gets the attention of God not because we are so good but because we have been made the righteousness of God through the righteous act of God's son Jesus at Calvary. That having been said, how do we overcome the battle inside and declare war against the enemy of our mind? We walk in the Spirit of life.

Galatians 5:24-25
❖ [24] And they that are Christ's have crucified the flesh with the affections and lusts. [25]If we live in the Spirit, let us also walk in the Spirit.

When we accepted Christ as our personal Savior we now have rights that stem from that relationship. Being born again means that I have a new set of parameters from which to operate. Paul says I delight in the law of God after the inward man. In other words there is something about this relationship with Christ that causes joy and hopefulness within us. It is restoring our reality of what life could have been prior to our fall as a human race. This delight Paul speaks of in Romans chapter 7:22 is tied to his new nature in Christ. His inward man knows that life is more than he has lived. The inward person has been transformed and longs for a higher dimension in God. "Paul" recognizes that "Saul" is still trying to talk to him from a dead place. Dr. C. I. Scofield D. D. says, "that the contrast is not between two methods of interpretation, which is literal and spiritual, but between two methods of divine healing: one through the law, the other through the Holy Spirit. (Scofield study Bible, pg1199) This insight suggest to us that in all of our attempts to be perfect using the law we cannot; because the law is perfect in itself and we are imperfect in ourselves. The tension that lies between it and us is literal. We change and it does not. We may seek to interpret the law in a favorable light so that we are less guilty but when all is said and done we are still inadequate while trying to live up to it's mandates. The law does not bend at all. It is what it is. And while it is what it is, it is still spiritual in that it upholds the mandates and commandments of God. God knew that we could in no wise live up to the perfection of the law, so God instituted the law of grace driven by our connection to the Holy Spirit. As Dr. Scofield says we have two methods of healing. Both methods work but for us the difference being one works better than the other. Because we have a tendency to fall and make mistakes, God has given us power through the Holy Spirit to overcome when we declare war. When we take this stand against our members we will glorify God in our body and in our spirits. We will act as living testimonies of God's triumphal work in us on behalf of His kingdom coming to earth. As a believer we are the dwelling place of God's Holy Spirit.

2 Cor. 6:14
- ❖ ¹⁴Be ye not unequally yoked together with unbelievers: for what fellowship hath righteousness with unrighteousness? and what communion hath light

with darkness? ⁱ⁵And what concord hath Christ with Belial? or what part hath he that believeth with an infidel? ¹⁶And what agreement hath the temple of God with idols? for ye are the temple of the living God; as God hath said, I will dwell in them, and walk in them; and I will be their God, and they shall be my people. ¹⁷Wherefore come out from among them, and be ye separate, saith the Lord, and touch not the unclean thing; and I will receive you. ¹⁸And will be a Father unto you, and ye shall be my sons and daughters, saith the Lord Almighty.

There are many things that affect a persons ability to confidently walk with God most of which has to do with what has influence over them. It is no secret that what we find important helps to establish how we operate in and for the world. We are driven to either maintain or accomplish goals based on what has influence over us. Much of the reasons for why we don't want to walk with God have to do with the people who hold influence in our lives. Sometimes they are relatives, coworkers, friends, social icons, or entertainment personalities. But whomever or whatever they may be, we are affected by their influence in our lives. What they think about issues and current world situations feed our disposition to make Godly choices. Just the other day I was reading an article from a guy who was fed up with the whole God thing. He grew up in the church and was made to participate in the process of church, but as he grew older he asked questions that he did not get answers for. In his mind we are the "Black Church Mafia" holding people hostage through mediums of ritual and worship. As I read the article, I began to think about what brought him to this place of God hatred and resentment for God's people. His brother was a prominent pastor and his mother had become a minister also before she died. In his mind God is irrelevant and unnecessary. He says that God is for people who are afraid and weak minded. His friends say that college caused the shift in his thinking but he says he just prefers not to be ignorant. But in the midst of his rambling I got a sense that someone of influence let him see a part of them that was not necessarily Godly. Their influence in his life drove him to be an atheist. Now he says, "if God wants to save me, He's knows right where I am."

A person is fooling themselves when they say that surroundings don't make a difference. You can not expect to be Godly associating with people who don't have a God conscious. It is somewhat like trying to push water up a hill. You may get a handle on the problem and look like you are about to solve the crisis. But eventually, the water reminds you that it has a mind all its own and will do as it pleases. There are people in our lives that we love and love us, but don't respect or represent a Godly mentality. These people may not mean you or I any ill will; but by virtue of their choice to not walk with God they pose a threat to our commitment to want to walk with God. It is a natural instinct to want to see them whole and living a blessed life, but remember you can't make anybody do anything for any length of time that they do not want to do. It is a futile journey. As believers we must be careful not to stay in places too long. I say again we must not lose our ability to say goodbye. In order to wage war for the territory of your mind, it is necessary at times to retreat in order to gain perspective. The text says be not unequally yoked together with unbelievers. Paul is essentially trying to get the church of Corinth to understand their position as children of God. They are the righteousness of God through Jesus Christ. Therefore they should not be in balance with entities that are not seeking righteousness. This does not mean they are not called to witness and share the saving work of Jesus Christ, but it does mean they must guard their lives against anything that would seek to alienate them or sway them from the affections of God. The literal definition of the term used by Paul concerning this type of relationship is not to have fellowship with one who is not an equal. I can't tell you how many times in my life I have had grief simply because I was with someone who was not my equal. Not because I was better in the formal sense but because of abilities and talents that I possessed. Because of where they were not, I incurred their disdain or contempt. I had done nothing to them out of order, but because of who I was and what was in me they had a problem and made it their business to give me the blues. In the body of Christ we are here for each other to strengthen, encourage, and enlighten for that sake of our walk with God. We are not each others enemies. We are equally yoke or in balance with each other. We make each other better in hopes of having grace and peace multiplied. In every situation we are seeking to be more like Christ for the sake of our Fathers Glory. Verse 16 -18 says:

> ❖ "[16]And what agreement hath the temple of God with idols? for ye are the temple of the living God; as God hath said, I will dwell in them, and walk in them; and I will be their God, and they shall be my people. [17]Wherefore come out from among them, and be ye separate, saith the Lord, and touch not the unclean thing; and I will receive you. [18]And will be a Father unto you, and ye shall be my sons and daughters, saith the Lord Almighty."

We come out from among them not because we are better than they are but because we have a different agenda. Our agenda involves their liberation. Our departure is for their deliverance. We are salt and light the preservative of God and what good is salt if it has lost it savor. It is good for nothing, but to be thrown out and trodden under foot. We must come out from among them. Not to look down on them, but to inspire and motivate them to rise, take up your beds of afflictions and walk. Because if God could change our reality and give us hope, surely goodness and mercy can do the same for them. We must have an Exodus; leave the Egypt's of our lives, and head with all do diligence to the promise land. For we are kingdom carriers and we can not produce life unless we abide in Him. Therefore WE DECLARE WAR on anything that impedes our desires to abide in Christ.

Chapter VI Being a Kingdom Carrier

What does it mean to be a kingdom carrier? God has endowed all of us who believe in His Son the power to have his presence abiding in our being. And because the Spirit of God abides in us He can not help, but have an affect on us. Now you know why when you committed that sin you felt so bad inside. It was not just guilt it was a sense of divine disappointment. The Holy Spirit was saying don't and you did. The Spirit creates in us a conviction that can not be denied or overlooked. His whole work is to perfect us for the task of proper adjudication or intercession. How we understand and process our world is the principle problem with why we struggle with ruler-ship. Our ministry from God is to share the story of reconciliation. We are not to lord over but to impart from a position of servant hood. We must have a posture to rightly divide the word of truth even if after having divided it we stand inadequate. The Holy Spirit's job is to bring us into all manner of truth, so we can be fit kingdom carriers.

Jesus said in the disciple's prayer; let thy kingdom come on earth as it is in heaven. In order for that expectation to become a reality the humanity in us must be created anew. That is why Jesus said to Nicodemus in John 3:3 "Except a person be born again they cannot see the kingdom of God." We are skewed. Meaning, we do life based on what we have come to understand as truth, but herein lays the problem. We were born into a place of sin and shaped in iniquity therefore our first instinct is to pursue solutions from this world's perspective. It is the only framework we have to draw from. So then our first inclination prior to the intervention of the Holy Spirit is flawed, no matter how noble the action. There must be a rebirthing that opens a doorway from where God is to where we are. Our faith in Jesus Christ acts as a conduit to provoke the Holy Spirit to birth us again. Our flesh loses its affects and the Spirit of God gains control. Once we have submitted to the influence of the Holy Spirit we now have the ability to be righteous before God and therefore the righteousness of God in the earth. It is from this position that we have the right to ask what we will. The attitude and nature of God is now at residence in us for the sake of the kingdom coming on earth. We are Kingdom Carriers.

I once heard Dr. Myles Munroe say, we are the Kingdom of **Servant** Kings. The implication of the title is that we are supposed to rule, but with a servant mentality. We are in charge but driven by a different passion. Remember, our purpose and desire is to be able to ask God to bestow His glory on us for the sake of His name and persona being glorified. We want provision for the sake of kingdom purpose. In order to accomplish this task we must be motivated by what shall be, rather than what is. Let me explain. Our Heavenly Father is obsessed with the condition of humanity. God yearns to have all of humanity delivered from destruction. This means not some, but all of humanity saved. His pursuit is our blessing. Because He pursues, we have a blessing with our name on it. Luke 19:1 one tells of a tax collector by the name of Zaccheus whose desire was to see Jesus. According to historical account, a tax collector gained their living through the Roman tax farming system. Tax farming was originally a Roman practice whereby the burden of tax collection was removed from the Roman State to private individuals or groups. In essence, these individuals or groups paid the taxes for a certain area and for a certain period of time, and then attempted to cover their outlay by collecting money or saleable goods from the people within that area.*(Howatson M. C.: Oxford Companion to Classical Literature, Oxford University Press, 1989)* The system was widely abused because tax farming was speculative, meaning that the private individual or group must invest their own money initially to pay off the tax debt, against the hope of collecting a larger sum. The right to collect taxes for a particular region would be auctioned every few years for a value that (in theory) approximated the tax available for collection in that region. The payment to Rome was treated as a loan and the publicani/publican or tax collector would receive interest on their payment at the end of the collection period. In addition, any excess (over their bid) tax collected would be pure profit for the tax collector. The principal risk to the publican was that the tax collected would be less than the sum bid. *(Wikipedia,* **This article does not cite any references or sources.** *April 2007)* So, then you can imagine the liberties that were taken by each tax collector in Roman culture to insure that they did not lose on the exchange. People felt about them the same way we feel about the IRS today. They did not like them because they felt they were greedy and took more than their share. So, when Jesus makes a special effort to come to Zacchaeus' house it was seen as a major sin considering his profession. Let's take a look at the text.

Luke 19

❖ ¹ Jesus entered Jericho and was passing through. ² A man was there by the name of Zacchaeus; he was a chief tax collector and was wealthy. ³ He wanted to see who Jesus was, but being a short man he could not, because of the crowd. ⁴ So he ran ahead and climbed a sycamore-fig tree to see him, since Jesus was coming that way. ⁵ When Jesus reached the spot, he looked up and said to him, "Zacchaeus, come down immediately. I must stay at your house today." ⁶ So he came down at once and welcomed him gladly. ⁷ All the people saw this and began to mutter, "He has gone to be the guest of a 'sinner.' "⁸ But Zacchaeus stood up and said to the Lord, "Look, Lord! Here and now I give half of my possessions to the poor, and if I have cheated anybody out of anything, I will pay back four times the amount."⁹ Jesus said to him, "Today salvation has come to this house, because this man, too, is a son of Abraham. ¹⁰ For the Son of Man came to seek and to save what was lost."

POINTS OF INTEREST

Zacchaeus' desire

1. Zacchaeus wanted to see Jesus
2. Zacchaeus was short and could not see because of the crowd
3. Zacchaeus ran ahead of the crowd and climbed a sycamore-fig tree
4. Zacchaeus' effort gets the attention of Jesus

Jesus sees his effort and responds

1. Jesus looked up and spoke
2. Zacchaeus come down immediately I must <u>stay</u> at your house today.

Why Praise

Zacchaeus' response to Jesus' request

1. Zacchaeus came down at once
2. Zacchaeus welcomed Jesus gladly

The religious people of the day

1. They saw exchange and muttered
2. He has gone to be the guest of a sinner

Zacchaeus next response

1. Stood up and said to the Lord
2. Look, Lord! Here and now I give half of my possessions to the poor
3. If I have cheated anybody out of anything, I will pay back four times the amount.

Jesus sees his effort and responds.

❖ ⁹ Jesus said to him, "Today salvation has come to this house, because this man, too, is a son of Abraham. ¹⁰ For the Son of Man came to seek and to save what was lost."

Notice that Jesus never addressed the crowd or their accusation of His intention for being in Zacchaeus' house. He let what was going to be act as His defense for being there. In the Lords final response in the text we see two things at work. First, we see His omniscience. Jesus' ability to know Zacchaeus' heart for wanting to see Him which is the power of the "shall be" at work. Second, we see the heart of a servant at work. Jesus' desire was to do the will of His Father. So in his response to Zacchaeus' reply Jesus says salvation has come to your house because you are a son of

Abraham. Why? Because it was a part of the Our Heavenly Fathers initial promise to Abraham in the book of Genesis that he was going to be a father of many nations. By faith, Zacchaeus became a son of God. Now it was the duty and responsibility of Jesus the Righteous Servant to carry out the wishes of His Father. What was and is the desire of our Heavenly Father? It is to seek and save the lost. The servant king must be about the saving of the lost for the sake of Gods divine purpose to deliver humanity from destruction. We were meant to be rulers, lenders and not borrowers, the head and not the tail, above and not beneath. But for what purpose, so that the kingdom of God could come to the earth. This is why it is essential that we are born again and not masquerade for social acceptance or some other degree of cultural elevation. The believer acts as God's agent for liberation and transformation. That is why we don't have time to pretend that we have submitted to the Spirit of God when we have not. The hour is late and the Lord is soon to come. You and I have people we love who have not come into the full revelation of what it means to be saved. As believers we have power to transform the world that comes out of our servant mentality. Let's look at Matthew chapter 25 beginning with verse 31.

> ❖ ³¹When the Son of man shall come in his glory, and all the holy angels with him, then shall he sit upon the throne of his glory: ³²And before him shall be gathered all nations: and he shall separate them one from another, as a shepherd divideth his sheep from the goats: ³³And he shall set the <u>sheep on his right hand</u>, but <u>the goats on the left</u>. ³⁴Then shall the King say unto them on his right hand, Come, ye blessed of my Father*, inherit the kingdom prepared for you from the foundation of the world:* ³⁵For I was an hungred, and ye gave me meat: I was thirsty, and ye gave me

drink: I was a stranger, and ye took me in: [36]Naked, and ye clothed me: I was sick, and ye visited me: I was in prison, and ye came unto me. [37]Then shall the righteous answer him, saying, Lord, when saw we thee an hungred, and fed thee? or thirsty, and gave thee drink? [38]When saw we thee a stranger, and took thee in? or naked, and clothed thee? [39]Or when saw we thee sick, or in prison, and came unto thee? [40]And the King shall answer and say unto them, Verily I say unto you, ***Inasmuch as ye have done it unto one of the least of these my brethren, ye have done it unto me.*** [41]Then shall he say also unto them on the left hand, Depart from me, ye cursed, into everlasting fire, prepared for the devil and his angels: [42]For I was an hungred, and ye gave me no meat: I was thirsty, and ye gave me no drink: [43]I was a stranger, and ye took me not in: naked, and ye clothed me not: sick, and in prison, and ye visited me not. [44]Then shall they also answer him, saying, Lord, when saw we thee an hungred, or athirst, or a stranger, or naked, or sick, or in prison, and did not minister unto thee? [45]Then shall he answer them, saying, Verily I say unto you, Inasmuch as ye did it not to one of the least of these, ye did it not to me. [46]And these shall go away into everlasting punishment: but the righteous into life eternal.

Herein lays a dangerous trap. It almost gives us a shortcut to our inheritance. The text suggests meeting the needs of people is the way to claim our inheritance. So, then we go about doing good deeds trying to work out our soul salvation to the neglect of personal character, morality and integrity. We hold other people accountable for what they do not do socially and so begin the effort to be righteous. However, we will meet the needs of people but won't develop Christian character. Not realizing or not willing to realize that we nullify the kingdom of God in us through our actions. There are many people who do good deeds and participate in social justice everyday, but don't have Christian character. They do good deeds and are hailed by culture as good people, but live perverted and distorted lives. Just as a point of interest, there are no easy ways to develop truly integriful or righteous character. It takes conscientious and consistent effort to break down sins affects in and on our lives.

Galatians 5:18-21
❖ [18]But if ye be led of the Spirit, ye are not under the law. [19]Now the works of the flesh are manifest, which are these; Adultery, fornication, uncleanness, lasciviousness, [20]Idolatry, witchcraft, hatred, variance, emulations, wrath, strife, seditions, heresies, [21]Envyings, murders, drunkenness, revellings, and such like: of the which I tell you before, as I have also told you in time past, *that they which do such things shall not inherit the kingdom of God.*

So then I not only have to treat people right but I have to be right myself. I can not live a social gospel to the neglect of an intimate relationship with Christ and submission to the Holy Spirit. The Spirit of God gives us the ability to do good works that glorify the Father and also establish righteousness in the earth. John chapter 14:23 says, "Jesus answered and said unto him, if a man love me, he will keep my words: and my Father will love him, and we will come unto him, and make our abode with him." There are a couple of things that caught my attention in the text. The first one being that Jesus used the word love me and not loves me as if to say that our love for Him should be settled before we begin the journey. Secondly, notice the language when it says we will make our abode with him. Jesus and the Father will live in us. Their disposition and attitude will become ours. But why do the Holy Father and His beloved son Jesus want to abide in us? Considering, they know exactly who and what we are. They love us. Love is the driving force behind what God does for us and what we should do for God. How will the Holy Father and His beloved son Jesus come to abide in us? Verse 26 gives us the answer. But the Comforter, which is the Holy Ghost, whom the Father will send in my name, he shall teach you all things, and bring all things to your remembrance, whatsoever I have said unto you. He is essentially saying to His disciples I am going to give you something that will empower you to recall, evaluate, and implement what I have taught you while I was with you. The Holy Spirit is sent in the name of God the Father and God the Son on behalf of us the Servant Kings to endow us with the ability to rule. Jesus is our King and we are his servants, but as for the world we are the kings of the earth endowed by the Holy Spirit with the capacity to rule with integrity, honor, justice, and purity. We must submit to the Spirits will so that the kingdom can come on earth as it is in heaven. To be filled with the Holy Spirit is not just so we can speak in an unknown language, but so that we can be the righteousness of God in the earth. Gods eternal purpose is to have us with Him forever. We must be taught so that we don't mess up things in our effort to be righteous, because sometimes in our intention to do what is right we miss the mark. Condemnation and pride set in and we are found wanting. People we should have kept we let go and people we should have sent to another servant king or laborer we kept too long. The Holy Spirit acts as a stabilizer to create conviction and motivation all at the same time. But remember, the process we go through is not to our discredit, but to our perfection. The Holy Spirit's work in us is to perfect us for the work of God's Kingdom. We are the Kingdom of servant Kings.

Revelation 1: 4-6

❖ ⁴John to the seven churches which are in Asia: Grace be unto you, and peace, from him which is, and which was, and which is to come; and from the seven Spirits which are before his throne; ⁵And from Jesus Christ, who is the faithful witness, and the first begotten of the dead, and **the prince of the kings of the earth**. Unto him that loved us, and washed us from our sins in his own blood, ⁶**And hath made us kings and priests unto God and his Father;** to him be glory and dominion for ever and ever. Amen

Chapter VII The Attitude of the Kingdom Carrier

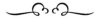

There is an attitude that comes with being in charge. It is a disposition of confidence and assurance that derives its origin from the creator of all things. Being a kingdom carrier means we must develop an attitude that suggests that in all things we have firm footing. We are not easily moved by situations or circumstances because we know in whom we have believed. But to suggest or infer that we are not human is to deny the condition that we are a part of. We are in the world, but not of this world. We are affected by the world that we live in simply because we are connected to it, but we overcome the world through our faith in the risen Christ. As the world looks at us it would seem to them that we are arrogant, overbearing, willful or stubborn, simply because we hold firm to our faith and are not easily moved. But the truth of the matter is that you and I are persuaded by our relationship to be full of faith. We know what God has done and is doing in our lives. To deny Him is to deny the love that was faithful to us even when we were faithless. God's love found us in a condition of hopelessness dreaming about things that would give us worldly satisfaction, but no eternal peace. It is not that we mean to assert we are better than anyone else just better off, because we have come to know the Christ and the indwelling of the Holy Spirit. We have been empowered to act as agents of social and spiritual change. We are kingdom carriers. The original background text for our discourse comes from John 17:1 where Jesus looks up to heaven and says, Father, the hour is come; glorify thy Son, that thy Son also may glorify thee. As the world looks in and overhears on our relationship with Jesus Christ they judge us for having exclusive rights to access God. They assume that we are putting down other people for their right to believe in their god and have access to their god. But what they don't understand is that we are not putting them down for having access to their god. They have a right to believe what they want to believe, but to assert that their belief system gives them access to our God is to deny the writings of our sacred scripture as trifles rather than eternal mandates and principles. So when Jesus says, "that I may glorify thee in the text" he is saying I am going to do my part by being a kingdom carrier and give my life for the cause and purpose of my Father, but I can't make you, the people, see my commitment as devotion if you choose to see it as arrogance or defiance of a particular social order. Jesus is saying I am willing to die because the relationship I have with my Father is worth it. When we lift our hands in adoration to God we can't make the world know how much we love Him. As we cry and suffer humiliation for the cause of Christ, we can't make them understand that it is not fear that restrains us but a Holy call to be different. When we shout uncontrollably and seem to have this fixation on things above that makes us look like we have lost our minds, we can't help that we are being ushered into His presence. We are in the process of developing an attitude like our elder brother. As believers we can not help what they say as we do our devotion to the Lord, but we can respond to their condition with the compassion of our Savior. To coin a popular musical phrase "People need the Lord." They just don't realize it yet and that is why we must be proper kingdom carriers. Paul says in 1 Corinthians 9:19-23:

> ❖ [19]For though I be free from all men, yet have I made myself servant unto all, that I might gain the more. [20]And unto the Jews I became as a Jew, that I might gain the Jews; to them that are under the law, as under the law, that I might gain them that are under the law; [21]To them that are without law, as without law, (being not without law to God, but under the law to Christ,) that I might gain them that are without law. [22]To the weak became I as weak, that I might gain the weak: I am made all things to all men, that I might by all means save some. [23]And this I do for the gospel's sake, that I might be partaker thereof with you.

As kingdom carriers we are not driven by our fascination to be wealthy or prosperous even though we have need of provision in order to be sustained in this world. We are motivated by our desire to see all people saved from the destruction prepared for those who do not believe. We don't condemn the world for their lack of belief because being without faith in Christ does that for them. Paul's temperament in the text is to do whatever he can to sway the mindsets of people to believe in the Christ because he knows that God is no respecter of person. If God spared not His only Son, what hope is there for the rest of the world if they do not lay hold to so great a gift? As God releases us into our divine rights as kings in the earth we must be able to rule well. We like Paul may not be able to win them all, but some of them will hear and obey. We are the Kingdom of Servant kings. John 13:3 cites an interesting encounter involving our King. It shows a particular behavior that if we are going to get our Heavenly Father to release His glory on our lives we must emulate.

Why Praise

> ❖ ³Jesus knowing that the Father had given all things into his hands, and that he was come from God, and went to God; ⁴He riseth from supper, and laid aside his garments; and took a towel, and girded himself. ⁵After that he poureth water into a bason, and began to wash the disciples' feet, and to wipe them with the towel wherewith he was girded.

Look at the posture of our King. The first thing we must recognize about our King is his posture did not diminish he station or position. Notice that the text said Jesus knowing that the Father had given all things into His hands and that he was come from God and went to God. This statement suggests that Jesus was secure in His identity. He was not going to be persuaded to be something less than He knew Himself to be. Whatever situation He chose to be in or found himself a part of, He did not relinquish his function or position as Son of God. Also note that Jesus made a deliberate effort to leave His place at the fellowship table, and lay aside His garments. As if to say even though I am King of kings and Lord of lords, I lay it all down to serve your condition. Jesus then proceeded to take a towel which in my mind was significant because it was something they could understand. It was from their context. Everybody has a towel or if you will an issue that needs addressing. Then Jesus proceeded to gird himself with it as if to say your issues are not too dirty for me. I am sent for matters just like these. Then the Water of Life pours water into a basin to give physical evidence of what would take place symbolically throughout the course of human history. He washed the disciples' feet as if to say to them, wherever you go from now on you are clean because of Me. We are forever connected because of what I have done to and for your condition. Jesus wiped their feet with His towel which for me also signifies His confidence in His station as Savior. Calvary was His issue and just like them we have been and will always be washed because of it. This whole episode shows the intention of the Savior to see after the condition of His disciples. They needed what He had to give. Jesus could have taken the attitude of let them come and get what they need. But He knew they had no idea they needed to be washed. So He took on the role of a servant king in order to meet a need. And if you and I are going to rule in this fashion, we must take on His attitude concerning the world we live in. In verse 12 Jesus gives reason for His actions.

> ❖ [12] So after he had washed their feet, and had taken his garments, and was set down again, he said unto them, Know ye what I have done to you?[13] Ye call me Master and Lord: and ye say well; for so I am. [14] If I then, your Lord and Master, have washed your feet; ye also ought to wash one another's feet. [15] For I have given you an example, that ye should do as I have done to you. [16] Verily, verily, I say unto you, The servant is not greater than his lord; neither he that is sent greater than he that sent him. [17] If ye know these things, happy are ye if ye do them.

The only weapon that the enemy has against the children of God is our fear of extinction. This does not mean death only, but the fear of loss from acquaintances that would affirm us as people. Once we conquer the spirit of fear then our place in life has been solidified. Our purpose is strengthened and we are made whole. While there is a healthy fear that governs stupid behavior we are not subject to a fear that cripples us from being all God intended. As believers we know God has not given us a spirit of fear but of power, love, and a sound mind. Therefore, in all things we await direction, deliverance, and destiny. All of which come as we participate in the will of God for us individually as well as for humanity collectively. The resource for our preservation and elevation is found in our thoughts and temperament concerning Jesus Christ. Not just the saving work of Calvary, because that was out of our hands, but the very fact that He is Lord of all. How we understand and process this all important concept is the mortar and brick of our confident lifestyle. Because the Lord is sovereign, there is no situation, issue, conflict, or peril that is outside of His jurisdiction. All things are given unto to Him. And because we believe in this, we reflect that image into the world. Our abilities, talents, and gifting take on a supernatural influence that transform and enlighten.

> 2 Corinthians 4:6-10 says:
> ❖ ⁶For God, who commanded the light to shine out of darkness, hath shined in our hearts, to give the light of the knowledge of the glory of God in the face of Jesus Christ. ⁷But we have this treasure in earthen vessels, that the excellency of the power may be of God, and not of us. ⁸We are troubled on every side, yet not distressed; we are perplexed, but not in despair; ⁹Persecuted, but not forsaken; cast down, but not destroyed; ¹⁰Always bearing about in the body the dying of the Lord Jesus, that the life also of Jesus might be made manifest in our body.

Jesus the Son of God is our King. His rule and reign begins in our heart. Before we can conquer any demonic affliction or hellish situation, we must lay to rest any doubt about where Jesus resides in our affections. Have you ever heard the saying that an animal can smell fear? The enemy we fight thrives on our insecurities and indecisiveness. The prince of this world, Lucifer by name, knows when we are caught between two affections. It is from this point of view that he seeks to exploit our weakness and gain influence in the earth. In 1 Peter chapter 5, Peter gives a wonderful description of what ought to take place in the lives of those who lead, but he says something in verse eight and nine that helps to make a point concerning our adversary.

> ⁸ Control yourselves and be careful! The devil, your enemy, goes around like a roaring lion looking for someone to eat. ⁹ Refuse to give in to him, by standing strong in your faith. You know that your Christian family all over the world is having the same kinds of suffering. (*THE HOLY BIBLE, NEW CENTURY VERSION*® Copyright © 2005 by Thomas Nelson, Inc.)

It is imperative we settle the issue of Jesus, because life will try us in ways that will make us question our place in Him. We must in all situations seek to control ourselves and be careful, because the devil is like a lion looking for someone to consume. In the book of Job we find him doing the same thing. The adversary was lurking around moving to and fro in the earth trying to find someone to take advantage of. His desire is to provoke us into believing that we are less than we are through our everyday struggles. That is why we must settle the issue of Jesus Christ in our minds, so we can have the power to walk in confidence. Jesus is the Christ the Sovereign Lord of the universe and the word made flesh. He was in the beginning with God. All things were made by him; and without him was not any thing made that was made. In him was life; and the life was the light of men. And the light shineth in darkness; and the darkness comprehended it not. He came unto his own, and his own received him not. But as many as received him, to them gave he power to become the sons of God, even to them that believe on his name: Which were born, not of blood, nor of the will of the flesh, nor of the will of man, but of God. And the Word was made flesh, and dwelt among us, and we beheld his glory, the glory as of the only begotten of the Father, full of grace and truth. (John 1:1-5, 11-14) In him, we live move and have our being. The way we gain access to our King and His resources is to resolve there is no other name given unto heaven where by people can be saved. He deserves our loyalty considering the price He paid to secure our freedom. And our King said in verse thirty four of John chapter thirteen, a new commandment I give unto you, that ye love one another; as I have loved you, that ye also love one another. By this shall all men know that ye are my disciples, if ye have love one to another. This is the attitude of the Kingdom Carrier.

Chapter VIII King Jesus

The principle reason why I have laid so much emphasis on the Lordship of Jesus Christ is, because if we settle His place in our lives we gain the influence of using His name with power. When we lay His Lordship to rest, the name of Jesus Christ becomes more than a theological premise or ideological concept. It becomes a way of life. Our belief in Him gives us the strength to abide in His word when our heart is fainting because of the journey. And it is in our abiding that you and I are made whole. If we are going to be productive in any true sense we must abide in Him. While we are kingdom carriers, sons and daughters of God, we are by nature inclined to do things by our lower self. When we have made a conscious choice to say yes to Christ and no to our own nature we by that choice make a decision to cooperate with God in the redemption of all creation. So that there are fewer hiccups in the plan, it is imperative that we be aware of our inclination to sin and fall short of the glory of God. Everyday we must be about the business of dying to self for the sake of our Father's purpose. I am not proposing some unrealistic pursuit that is not attainable, but one that comes out of our new nature as children of God. Inherent in our new nature is the tools from which we find our God destiny. It is a lifestyle centered on what is important to God and by default we find what is important to us.

We come to understand that there are more important things in life than just provision. Once we lose the fear of life itself we gain strength and perspective that enables us and not stifles us. John chapter 14 verse 1 says, "let not your heart be troubled: ye believe in God believe also in me." This declaration by our Christ should confirm our conviction to abide in him. The text gives credence to the validity of who Christ is. Jesus makes a direct connection from Himself to God the creator in hopes of strengthening the trust of His followers. But before He attaches Himself to God the Father, He gives us a piece of peace through his statement. He says, "Let not you heart be troubled." I can not tell you how many times I have spoken that phrase to myself in confidence God knew exactly where I was and what I was going through. It has helped to reassure me that I am not alone in the process of life and that Christ cares. Verse two and three of the same chapter once again connects Jesus with the provision and perspective of His Father. It reads: In my Father's house are many mansions: if it were not so I would have told you. I go to prepare a place for you. And if I go and prepare a place for you, I will come again, and receive you unto myself; that where I am, there ye may be also.

One of the principle reasons why you and I can find refuge and confidence in the Christ is his disposition to care about our condition. There is always this unrelenting desire to have us with him in His Fathers house. Christ's leaving was predicated on His responsibility or desire to prepare a place for us in His Fathers' house. All that Jesus went through was to secure our place with God. So then, the work of Jesus was not just about provision, but relationship. The primary purpose of Jesus Christ, while he took away our sins through His sacrifice, was to reconnect or re-establish our relationship to the Heavenly Father. The act of Calvary took care of our sins, but the commitment of Jesus to the purpose of His Father assured us that we would always have a place in the Father's house. Our lives as believers would be nothing without the relationship we have gained through our brother's sacrifice. Jesus says of himself in verse six "I am the way, the truth, and the life: no man cometh unto the Father but by me." We gain access to a life worth living when we recognize the significant role Jesus plays in the economy of God. I am the way represents processes that empower us to do works of righteousness. He is the road we must travel to produce fruits worthy of God. Jesus is the course of conduct that transforms any and every culture. Acceptance of Jesus Christ as the way puts us on the road to intimacy with our Heavenly Father. But if that was not enough, Jesus goes on to say the he is also the truth. What truth? Truth in and of itself is relative to the person that speaks it. Just because someone says they are telling the truth does not mean that it is absolute. Their truth is relative to their interpretation of whatever account of events they witnessed. In other words depending on how they felt when they witnessed the event, their account could be tainted by their own bias. But because Christ is connected to the Father of all creation, by being the living word made flesh, He has not just a truth, but the truth. Jesus is the true notions of God revealed. This truth is established in his person as the Savior of humanity. His truth gets us into the presence of Almighty God like a key to a locked door. Because of this truth, we all have the opportunity to experience life at a different level. It is a life of freshness and reoccurring newness. We are made over again and again and again. Our obstacles don't take us down, but lift us to a more persuaded place. By believing in the witness of Jesus Christ our again never stops and we are transmuted into that place not made by hands. Ultimately, it is the place where our mortality puts on immortality and our corruptible puts on incorruption. It is the place where darkness has been swallowed up in light and there is no more night. In the words of the late Mahalia Jackson, it is a place where everyday is "howdy howdy." In Jesus Christ we have a living witness to the presence and demeanor of God. Jesus is not just a cultural icon or some super spiritual medicine man, He is God's act of redeeming humanity from the rebellion within. Jesus is grace at work from God the Father to us the fallen creature. Everything that we are as Christians lay at the feet of this conviction. We must know that we are not forsaken or forgotten when we fail at the process. Grace keeps us in place to continue the work in spite of our imperfections. The belief that God is on our side working through Jesus' act at Calvary gives us access to His perspective, decision making, and provision. John Chapter 14 beginning at verse 12 says:

> ❖ [12]Verily, verily, I say unto you, He that believeth on me, the works that I do shall he do also; and greater works than these shall he do; because I go unto my Father. [13]And whatsoever ye shall ask in my name, that will I do, that the Father may be glorified in the Son. [14]If ye shall ask any thing in my name, I will do it.

Notice that the blessing of the text hangs on our utter belief in the person and actions of Jesus Christ. Not just the philosophy or ideology of Jesus but the very essence of who and what He was and is. If we can get ourselves to believe in Him absolutely in every situation and circumstance we get the rare opportunity to do what Jesus did and then some. This is why we must get over whether or not Jesus is in charge of our lives because He left us with the responsibility to be transformers. Jesus changed the landscape of time itself. He was more than a figure. He was a force. As believers we are supposed to have the same affect. If we can lay to rest the doubt and the suspect questions over who Jesus was, what Jesus did, and where Jesus came from we can ask what we will in His name. This is the turning point. This is the axis.

This is the crossroad. To have the ability to ask what we will. When we settle the issue of Jesus Christ and believe in Him in the face of all else we get the privilege to live and not die. Why? Because when we ask and the Father answers, it solidifies the relationship between the righteous servant and His Lord. In the Book of Isaiah Chapter 53 verse 11 there is a reference to the act of Gods Righteous Servant justifying many and fulfilling the work of God in the earth by bearing their iniquities. Verse 12 makes a statement relative to the act of the righteous servant. It says:

- ❖ [12]Therefore will I divide him a portion with the great, and he shall divide the spoil with the strong; because he hath poured out his soul unto death: and he was numbered with the transgressors; and he bare the sin of many, and made intercession for the transgressors.

When we ask what we will it is not just a request tied to our need but a portion of the spoil or treasure divided to those who believe in the act of the Righteous Servant. His righteous act was to pour out His soul unto death and be numbered with the transgressors. In my mind, the Isaiah text makes a direct connection to John 14 verse 13 when Jesus says, "whatsoever ye shall ask in my name, that will I do, that the Father may be glorified in the Son." Jesus is inextricably tied to His Fathers directive and we are inextricably tied to Jesus and His place in God. Therefore whatever we ask in Christ glorifies our Heavenly Father and the relationship God has with Jesus His Son. Our asking in the name of Jesus puts God in the position to answer. And when God answers, it puts us in the position to give Him glory for having heard our request. God getting glory is the reason for our existence. Isaiah 43:7 says, "even every one that is called by my name: for I have created him for my glory, I have formed him; yea, I have made him."

Sometimes I hear people who have no real reverence for God say things that border on blasphemy. They make statements like: What kind of God needs to be praised and patted on the back for every little thing He does? Your God must be suffering from a self esteem problem if we are to spend our time always letting Him know how wonderful He is. The problem with statements like these is that they are an attempt on the part of people to provoke God into showing off His power. God does not have to prove His prowess or power. He just waits for a situation or illness in life where money, resources, skill, savvy, ability, talent, influence, or who we know won't make the problem go away. God waits on us to cry "Abba Father." And it is at those moments that we come to know why He is called God alone. For when He answers all doubt is laid to rest and everything is made clear. God is God and there is none like Him. And like children who understand the blessing of good parents, we should give Him praise. We celebrate the opportunity to tell God thank you. It is in our thank you or our grateful response that we get Gods attention and are glorified. But why are we so thankful for the opportunity to ask? We love Him. The old church used to sing a song that says "I love the Lord He heard my cry and pitied every groan and Long as I live and trouble rise I'll hasten to His throne." Why do we run to Him? Why do we cry to Him? Why do we look to Him? Because, we love Him for all He is to us in our condition. God hears us because He loves us.

Love is the glue of our relationship. It is what constrains us, drives us, inspires us and motivates us to action. Knowing that we are loved in such a profound way provokes and convicts us to love God back. Love is the affection that stimulates our Father to hear our request. And because we have such a shallow view of love as a culture we dismiss His love as a trinket rather than a precious heirloom. John 3:16 says it well, for God so loved the world, that he gave his only begotten Son, that whosoever believeth in him should not perish, but have everlasting life. We do not perish because God loves us. The evidence of our commitment to God's love is when we keep His words. Not just his commandments in the literal sense, but His very words for doing life and relationship with people in general. According to John 14:23 love caused Jesus Christ and God the Father to make their abode with us.

- ❖ ²³Jesus answered and said unto him, If a man love me, he will keep my words: and my Father will love him, and we will come unto him, and make our abode with him.

The word abode in the text literally means to make within us a dwelling place. It is our Fathers pleasure to be in us actively reaching the world through our love. So then, if we are going to get into a position that releases the resources of God we must love. Keeping the words of Christ causes God the Father to love us intimately, come unto us and dwell in us. This is the position of trustworthiness. Now we can be trusted to be glorified. The love of our lives directs what we ask so that we are not out of His will but in Him pursuing all things. For in Him we live move and have our being.

Chapter IX Absolute Devotion

Our love for Jesus Christ has brought us to a place where we can be trusted. The love we have for the ways of God have caused the presence of the Father and Son to take up residence in our hearts. This indwelling is made possible through the power of the Holy Spirit. God made a commitment that if His son would suffer the horrors of Calvary, that God would redeem humanity and save us from our sins through the act. Jesus says even though I am committed to your condition as a humanity I cannot be with you in all places, but my word can. So, in order to maintain what I have in you, I must go so the Father can send one charged with the responsibility to empower you through my words. The Holy Ghost shall teach you, guide you, direct you, comfort you and convict you of your sins, so that you will always remain in me. In order to be glorified we must abide. Our conscious decisions to abide in Jesus Christ gives us access to the ability of producing fruits that glorify God our Father. The key to a meaningful, productive and blessed life is to abide in Christ. As a people we have problems abiding in Him because of other tugs for our affection. There are many distractions that inflict their power of persuasion in an attempt to get us to choose them over doing the works of God. But in order to be affective in the work as a Christian, we must have a galvanized dedication to Him above all else.

That is why it is so important to fall in love with Jesus Christ and never waver in that conviction. That conviction sets the stage for our staying power in the midst of a heart that may want to give up on the process. I liken the relationship of the believer to that of a marriage between a husband and a wife. There are many tempting distractions in the world. At every turn we are being bombarded by images that reinforce the notion of infidelity. These images work on the inclinations of people to participate in marital infidelity, to anesthetize or dull the pain of having a broken heart or being disappointed. If we are not convicted over the relationship then we find more and more ways to justify why we should leave. This concept is also true of our relationship with Christ. If we prayed and asked God for something and God said no or not yet, then we are challenged to stay true to our commitment even though we feel let down and ignored. Christ demands absolute loyalty and dedication. Matt. 10: 37-38 says:

> ❖ ³⁷He that loveth father or mother more than me is not worthy of me: and he that loveth son or daughter more than me is not worthy of me. **38**And he that taketh not his cross, and followeth after me, is not worthy of me.

Once you make a choice to put Christ at the center of all things you can expect to have some tension in your everyday relationships. Our devotion and affection for Him can make people feel like they are in competition with Christ for our affections. If they are close relatives or immediate household members then they feel abandoned and forsaken. This tug of war can reek havoc on our commitment to serve the Lord with our whole heart, because we have a desire to maintain our prior relationships in their original capacity. But when we come into the full knowledge of Jesus Christ, everything in our lives must change. The relationship with Christ demands

Why Praise

it. It is indeed a burden to carry the disappointment of others as we develop our Christian way of life but if we are going to ask what we will from the Father we have got to figure out who and what we want most, them or Him. This is the cross we must bear. In the book of Mark 8:27 there is an account of Jesus asking His disciples whom do people say that I am that gives credence to what it takes to follow and abide.

Mark 8:27-38

❖ ²⁷And Jesus went out, and his disciples, into the towns of Caesarea Philippi: and by the way he asked his disciples, saying unto them, Whom do men say that I am? ²⁸And they answered, John the Baptist; but some say, Elias; and others, One of the prophets. ²⁹And he saith unto them, But whom say ye that I am? And Peter answereth and saith unto him, Thou art the Christ. ³⁰And he charged them that they should tell no man of him. ³¹And he began to teach them, that the Son of man must suffer many things, and be rejected of the elders, and of the chief priests, and scribes, and be killed, and after three days rise again. ³²And he spake that saying openly. And Peter took him, and began to rebuke him. ³³But when he had turned about and looked on his disciples, he rebuked Peter, saying, Get thee behind me, Satan: for thou savourest not the things that be of God, but the things that be of men. ³⁴And when he had called the people unto him with his disciples also, he said unto them, Whosoever will come after me, let him deny himself, and take up his cross, and follow me. ³⁵For whosoever will save his life shall lose it; but whosoever shall lose his life for my sake and the gospel's, the same shall save it. ³⁶For what shall it profit a man, if he shall gain the whole world, and lose his own soul? ³⁷Or what shall a man give in exchange for his soul? ³⁸Whosoever therefore shall be ashamed of me and of my words in this adulterous and sinful generation; of him also shall the Son of man be ashamed, when he cometh in the glory of his Father with the holy angels.

Jesus starts with a question of identity. Jesus knows who he is, but what He wants to know is do they know who He is. Out of this text we get the great prophetic announcement that Jesus is the Christ the son of the Living God. But in the midst of all this spiritual revelation comes this very human and earthly concern from Peter for the safety of Jesus as He does ministry. Jesus was telling His disciples of His coming suffering, but Peter was caught up in his affection for Jesus rather than the Lords mission and calling. In Matthew chapter 16 verse 22 we get a sense of Peter's struggle with letting Jesus do what He was called to do. "Peter took Jesus aside and told him not to talk like that. He said, "God save you from those things, Lord! Those things will never happen to you!"(New Century Version) Jesus loved Peter, but at that moment Peter let his love for Jesus cloud his vision. Jesus had to bring Peter's vision back into focus. Jesus, said to Peter get thee behind me Satan. This may seem harsh considering the fact that Jesus loved Peter. But at the moment there was another agenda at work in the heart of Peter. Even though Jesus loved Peter, Jesus loved His Fathers purpose and will for His life more. It was not a question of love and affection for Peter, but a statement of commitment to His Father. At that point Jesus had to make a choice between His friend Peter and His Father who was God. Because Jesus had already settled the issue of where His affection lie when it came time to choose between earthly relationships and His Heavenly Father the choice was already decided. After He finished dealing with Peter, Jesus proceeded to explain so that His actions would not seem malicious. It is critical for us that we understand that God is not against earthly relationships; If He was, then

God would not have put us in relationship to others. The thing we have to learn how to balance in our lives is the significance we place on those earthly relationships. Christ knew His purpose for coming to earth. And while Christ was moved by the sentiment from Peter, it was inappropriate for His life because it would make Him cling to this world rather, than look unto the next. Notice in verse 33 how after telling Satan to get behind him, Jesus says, "for thou savourest not the things that be of God, but the things that be of men." This statement brings into clarity the mindset of the believer. If we are going to be able to ask what we will, then we must change our focus. The word savor for me has a cooking or dining overtone to it. In that, it implies we ought to let the purpose of God marinade in us like the wine taster who sloshes fine wine around in their mouth to get the full affect of the flavor, or the food taster who does not swallow too quickly but takes their time trying to pick out every little spice. Sometimes the flavor is sweet and other times it is tart or sour. But in any case, it is still the flavor of the wine or the food the taster is seeking to experience. As we walk with God, it can be just like that sometimes, but in the end it is the Lord that we are trying to experience and duplicate. You and I must develop the art of denial. My Dad had a saying he used to use on us when we wanted something he didn't think we should have. Daddy would say, "Everything that looks good to you is not good for you." Remember when I said that we should not lose the art of saying goodbye. Here is another one to catalog. Learn how to say no, to yourself. There are many things that keep us from walking with God in spirit and in truth. It is this dualistic devotion that keeps us from asking what we will and having the confidence that God is going to answer our prayer. We love God in our spirit but the truth is that we are still hanging on to this world too closely, and have not learned how to say no and mean it. We are too easily swayed by other influences. The spirit is willing, but the flesh is weak. When we would do good evil is always present. We all have sinned and fallen short of the glory of God. All of these scriptures are true in their own right, but really they only create a comfortable place for us to continue the habit of not saying, no. When we choose not to say no, it works against our desire to abide in Christ. Saying no creates stability, structure, discipline and courage. What really happens is that we develop single-mindedness as to what is most important about life. We are tempted on every side, but the power of our conviction for Christ should motivate us to say no. When we overcome our temptation moments we are working on a faith that can stand through the everyday rigors of life. James chapter 1;2-3 says:

❖ ²My brethren, count it all joy when ye fall into divers temptations; ³Knowing this, that the trying of your faith worketh patience. ⁴But let patience have her perfect work, that ye may be perfect and entire, wanting nothing.

Denying ourselves helps to establish patience, so while we wait on God to answer our prayer we do not lose heart and perish for lack of belief. Patience creates in us a discipline for waiting on God. And while we wait, our faith is increased; we are perfected and are taught in whatever state we are in to be content. We are assured God knows what we have need of. Denying ourselves gets us in touch with the divine order of life meaning that Jesus denied His place in Glory just to save us from our condition. When we deny ourselves, we are teaching our fleshly desires that we are governed by a higher consciousness. This consciousness puts emphasis on what is heavenly and not earthly. The condition of our soul becomes our primary concern even though we are in need of provision. That is what Jesus meant when He said, in verse 36 and 37 of Mark 8, "for what shall it profit a man, if he shall gain the whole world, and lose his own soul? 37Or what shall a man give in exchange for his soul?" The appetite of the soul is what gets the attention of God because our outward actions don't always speak the truth about what is in our heart. If the intentions of our heart are to walk with God then more than likely in our everyday pursuit's life will mimic that sentiment. It is imperative we work on our soul condition so we gain strength for the journey of life. Our physical condition takes on a new context when we look at it through the eyes of faith. Why do I deny my flesh? I am trying to gain a heavenly crown. There is more to life than what we see. Our ability to abide in Christ is centered on our commitment to seek Him first. Out of this devotion we get the blessing of the promise. Seek first the kingdom of God and its righteousness and all these things shall be added unto you. In other words if I can make myself develop the art of saying no to others as well as myself then I lay hold to the unending resources of God. As a believer I can't bear fruit worthy of God unless I can say no when it is necessary. Why do I say no? So I can stay in the vine. If I stay in the vine then I can ask what I will.

Chapter X Being Holy and Being Human

In the book "Being Holy and, Being Human Dealing with the expectations of ministry" by Jay Keasler, in the opening statement of his book he asserts, and I quote; Holy and human. Can anyone be both? In many ways, being holy and being human is a contradiction in terms. Yet that is the challenge facing every Christian leader.

As Christians, we're to be holy — set apart, sanctified, pure. As human beings, however, we confess a not-so-flattering truth: we are *not* holy. Never have been. Never will be, at least this side of eternity. (Kesler, Jay: *Being Holy, Being Human: Dealing With the Expectations of Ministry.* Carol Stream, Ill.; Waco, Tex.: CTI; Word Books, 1988 (The Leadership Library 13), S. 9) As I listen to Mr. Kesler I am drawn to the profundity or depth of his statement regarding our dilemma to be all God requires. It is a tension that every believer has struggled with since the day they said yes to Jesus and no to the world. We are caught in the vice grip of flesh and blood. And he is right when he says that being holy and being human seems to be a contradiction in terms, but here is where I take issue. God does not leave the holiness to our humanness which is frail, subject to imperfections, filled with inclinations of iniquity, but to his divine economy of

Why Praise

saving grace and Spirit indwelling. The ability to live holy is not ours alone for if it were the challenge would be too great a burden to bear. There are many people who try daily not to mess up, only to find out that they are just human and what God says concerning people in Genesis 6:5 is true *that every imagination of the thoughts of their heart was* only evil continually. And being human means falling short of Gods glory. This by no means gives us the right to not work at the process of holiness and develop the talent for saying no, but it does bring into perspective the nature of our condition. Our holiness is an act of God on behalf of His desire to be with us. Our legalistic mindsets will only engender in us what Christ came to liberate us from. We are more than what we do. We are the sum total of what we do and what we have the potential to do. God through the act of Christ has endowed us with the potential to be more than sinners. We can be Saints. In our humanness we are subject to sin but in our sainthood we have this treasure in earthen vessels that what happens in us is from God and not us. The only requirement from God for this process to continue is for us to have the desire to abide in Him. When we abide in Christ we are given access to the provisions of His name sake. John Chapter 15 beginning with verse 1 says:

> ❖ ¹ I am the true vine, and my Father is the husbandman. ² Every branch in me that beareth not fruit he taketh away: and every *branch* that beareth fruit, he purgeth it, that it may bring forth more fruit. ³ Now ye are clean through the word which I have spoken unto you. ⁴ Abide in me, and I in you. As the branch cannot bear fruit of itself, except it abide in the vine; no more can ye, except ye abide in me. ⁵ I am the vine, ye *are* the branches: He that abideth in me, and I in him, the same bringeth forth much fruit: for without me ye can do nothing.

If we are going to be effective in our lives as believers we must make a conscious decision to stay in Christ no matter what. If not, we will quickly begin to feel the futility of our decision. Jesus says I am the vine. Whatever we need can be found in Christ. The symbolism is profound in that, we know all of the ingredients necessary for fruit to grow are found in the vine. But the vines transport of the ingredients for the fruit is only as effective as the branches connection to the vine. So then, if we are half connected then we only get partially what we need to grow. Jesus is fully connected to His Father, so we should be fully connected to Jesus. The whole reason for our connection to Christ is to produce fruit worthy of God's glory. Christ redeemed us for the sole purpose of bringing God glory. Note in the text that God is the husbandman and that it is His responsibility to deal with fruit production. There are two categories: one that does not bear fruit and the one that bears fruit. If we are not bearing fruit, we are taken away, but if we are bearing fruit it is God's responsibility to make us bear more fruit. In verse two, we see the word purge which essentially means to cleanse of filth or impurity. This act is not just a one time experience but a continual cleansing that God takes responsibility for everyday of our lives. In other words it has happened; It is happening; And it will happen. His power to make us productive is only stifled by our decision not to submit to His will. We fight Gods purging because our humanness seeks to hold on to our fallen state. Here is the tension of being human and being holy. Which one do we want more? If we submit to the purging process then our humanity takes on a more lofty ideal and we are made useful for the glory of God, but if we digress and fall prey to the temptation to live in our humanity then we are a people most miserable. We were created to bring God glory and any time we are not living out that purpose we are living beneath our privilege as human beings. We are not here just to have pleasure. Or are we? Pleasure is relative. I have always heard

Why Praise

the saying that "Some folk's pleasure is other folk's pain." This is true. 1 Corinthians 1:18 bears witness to this fact. "For the preaching of the cross is to them that perish foolishness; but unto us which are saved it is the power of God." For some people preaching is a waste of time to others it is the inspiration that keeps them from giving up. When God created us in Eden our lives were filled with the pleasure of life itself. We lived in paradise with no worries other than the joy of daily fulfillment. Our pleasure was to be with God and each other. The relationships we had were our joy and peace. We were content being in harmony with nature through our servant hood to the garden. Work was not something we were trying to get away from but something that was a part of our job description as created beings. Gods design for us was enough to give us pleasure. When Satan came he created in us questions about our existence and our place in God. It was at that juncture we begin to understand pleasure from a different context. We began to question whether or not it was and is beneficial to abide or stay with God. Pleasure for us became something of a different sort. Now, we must have continual events to keep us happy or give us pleasure. We find purpose in what we have rather than who we are. It is not enough to be with God and know that we are living out a divine purpose. Now, we need to know what we are going to get out of the deal. So we struggle to stay in God because we think we are missing out on something more spectacular than what God has to offer. For the believer, our pleasure and purpose comes through the decision to say, "Father You Know Best." At that point we both lose and gain at the same time. Mark 8: 35 rings clear: For whosoever will save his life shall lose it; but whosoever shall lose his life for my sake and the gospel's, the same shall save it. We cease to be pawns in the chess game of life because by our active decision to abide in Christ, we have tilted the scales in our favor for all times. Even if tragedy comes we are still victorious because

Why Praise

we know this too shall pass. But why must the believer abide in Christ? Verse 5 of John 15 gives us the answer. I am the vine, ye *are* the branches: He that abideth in me, and I in him, the same bringeth forth much fruit: for without me ye can do nothing. We do not produce of ourselves. This is a hard reality to come to grips with because it means in all things we must give credit to someone or something else. Our abilities, skills, talents, or knowledge came from another entity other than ourselves. And no matter what we decide to do with them later we must always remember the slogan "we are only as tall as the shoulders we stand on." We are connectional creatures. Everything that we do can be attached to someone else. As human beings we struggle with this concept because what we do helps to validate us as valuable. In our eyes, the more we can do the more valuable we are. So we don't want to give that validation away because if we do we are no longer worth the consideration of others. We get looked over for someone else more gifted. So we struggle with giving up the praise. It is at this perspective we began our journey. Who do we throw the praise to? Who we throw the praise to determines how high we will go in life. Luke 14:11 says, "For whosoever exalteth himself shall be abased; and he that humbleth himself shall be exalted." So then praise is my attempt to say to God I did not get here alone. If it had not been for your guidance, patience, and tender mercy, life would have consumed me long ago. But because of your plan for my life and your purpose for me in spite of it all, I made it. The song writer was right when they said:

- ❖ Without God I can do nothing
  Without Him I fail.
  Without Him I would be broken like a ship without sail.

However, when we say "Father You Know Best" we are giving God the license to take His rightful place as creator.

The acknowledgement of our inability does two things. First, it reminds us of our constant need of God and the wisdom that only comes from God. Two, it tells God we are committed to staying in Him so that we can reach our assigned purpose. When we know our place it keeps us present and not absent in the learning process of life. God can use us because we want to be used. God does not have to force feed us like children who hate to eat their vegetables. As a believer we should always be in pursuit of knowing more about what God wants from us. If we have arrived in our attainment of knowledge then we have nothing else to learn. Therefore, we have no need of God because we are self sustaining. Again, this opens the door for pride and arrogance to set in. Proverbs 16:18 says, Pride *goeth* before destruction, and an haughty spirit before a fall. Pride in the negative sense is closely associated with conceit which essentially means an excessive appreciation of one's own worth or virtue. (Merriam-Webster, Inc: *Merriam-Webster's Collegiate Dictionary.* 10th ed. Springfield, Mass., U.S.A.: Merriam-Webster, 1996, c1993) That was the danger the tree of knowledge of good and evil posed to humanity. It gave us an excessive appreciation of our own worth and virtue. Because we now have a sense of the particulars good and evil pose, we are strained to find worth in service to God or even recognizing His significance in our lives. In our estimation, we can do well without the endorsement or intuition of God. This coupled with our need to be valuable puts us in the position to portray ourselves as demigods rather than beings dependent upon God. And when this mythological character flaw is a part of our makeup, it will cause us to separate from the vine. It is a false sense of power. Because God gave us the ability to gather knowledge, we sometimes think that we

Why Praise

got it on our own rather than realizing that God created an atmosphere for us to gain knowledge.

According to Wikipedia.org, the word serendipity is the effect by which one accidentally discovers something fortunate, especially while looking for something else entirely. In my estimation this is God creating an atmosphere for knowledge to expose itself so, that we can capitalize on its benefits. For instance, Chef George Crum made the interesting discovery of potato chips after a customer complained to him about his potato fries being cut way too thick. Being a wise guy he sliced a potato paper thin and then fried it to a crisp. The diner loved it, thus creating the world's very first potato chip. Potato Chips were they on purpose or by accident. A Scottish scientist named Alexander Fleming was looking into a cure for the flu in 1928 when he noticed that a blue-green mold had infected one of his Petri dishes, and it had killed the staphylococcus bacteria that had been growing in it. The world's most effective cure was actually discovered due to a contamination in the lab. What a unique coincidence! Penicillin, was it on purpose or by accident. Vulcanization of rubber, by Charles Goodyear. He accidentally left a piece of rubber mixture with sulfur on a hot plate, and produced vulcanized rubber. Vulcanized rubber, was it on purpose or by accident. Corn flakes and wheat flakes (Wheaties) were accidentally discovered by the Kelloggs brothers in 1898, when they left cooked wheat untended for a day and tried to roll the mass, obtaining a flaky material instead of a sheet. (Wikipedia.com) Corn Flakes was it on purpose or by accident. Artificial sweeteners were discovered in much the same way as penicillin. Three of them, Saccharin, Cyclamate, and Aspartame were all discovered in a one hundred year time period, and all by scientists who forgot to wash their hands after an experiment. Artificial sweeteners, was it on purpose or by accident. (www.thrifter.com) Humanity being what it is has learned how to take credit for what God reveals. The revelations of God are for our good, but they also represent an opportunity for us to give God praise for the atmosphere that produced the blessing. Our emotional strain over who should get the glory essentially tells God that we are not ready to operate in His glory. When we abide in Christ and the word of God abides in us it cleans and prunes us for the work of ministry reminding us of the necessity of God. If the Word of God is allowed to have free course in us then we can ask what we will and it shall be done. Why? Verse 8 of John chapter 15 gives us the answer. Herein is my Father glorified, that ye bear much fruit; so shall ye be my disciples. The whole reason for answered prayer, divine revelation, and God's abiding presence is so that the Father will be glorified. Does this mean that God does not care about what we are going through or what we are praying for? No. But it does remind us that there is a bigger purpose behind our answered prayers. There is more to an answered prayer than our breakthrough and comfort level. Just the other day I was giving my testimony to a gentleman and he began to cry. I told him how God had sustained me through my transition from Hot Springs, AR to Martin, TN. I gave him the particulars of my faith journey and how God had been faithful to His call for me and my wife to leave. Just hearing my testimony provoked him to become more faithful in seeking God's direction for his life. What God did for me was for me but not necessarily about me. God had some other folks in mind when He blessed me because God knew I could not keep it to myself.

2 Peter 3:9 says, The Lord is not slack concerning his promise, as some men count slackness; but is longsuffering to us-ward, not willing that any should perish, but that all should come to repentance. This verse reminds us that God keeps His word. Unlike humanity God will not lie. But thankfully, the nature of God is seated in His love and mercy. God suffers with us as we feel our way through the maze

of life. People focus on what we do wrong. God's focus is on what we can do right. The text also tells us that the primary purpose of God for humanity is that no one is lost. Because God is longsuffering to us-ward, we get the chance to repent, be saved and be used as a witness to others in order that they might be saved. The purpose of Gods glory in the life of the believer is so that people can come to know the Christ and the life connected to Him. Every time God answers our call it tells the world that God is not dead, but actively working on our behalf as Father suggesting that God is providing a means of escape. When we tell them that our breakthrough was because God heard our cry then they come to know there is a God indeed and that He really does care about their condition. Just as a side note. That is why it is so important for us as believers not to get caught up in the miracles, but in the relationship. If God stopped answering our prayers so that we saw no miracles, would our devotion to and for Him keep us actively praising Him? There is a song that says, "because of who you are I give you glory, because of who you are I give you praise, because of who you are I will lift my voice and say, Lord I worship you just for who you are." Miracles are only a small part of what God uses to cause people to repent and come unto Him. But the greatest tool God has for changing the world is the witness of His people. It is the abiding relationships that we form through the Holy Spirit that keep us connected in spite of our circumstances. That is why Job says, "though they slay me, yet will I trust Him." God's glory in the life of the believer is about trusting our heavenly Father above all else. In this process God is glorified and the unbeliever comes to know Jesus Christ through our witness. When we say yes to the Father, we are saying yes to all that concerns Him. So then, if we don't learn how to say no to ourselves, then we will never be able to abide or stay in Christ because everything else will seem to be more attractive. No is a prerequisite for abiding in Christ. Not because we don't want some things, people, or certain situations, but because we want Christ more. When we say no, we are essentially saying yes to being a disciple of Christ. In John chapter 15 beginning with verse 7 Jesus says, if ye abide in me, and my words abide in you, you shall ask what ye will, and it shall be done unto you. This can be a bit much to take considering all of the times we ask God for stuff by way of prayer, but Jesus said ask what you will and it shall be done. If we can learn how to abide at all cost, our breakthrough is at hand. But don't forget timing. Just because you ask for it now does not mean that you are going to get it now. The atmosphere must be conducive for that prayer to be answered. As the late G.E. Patterson used to say, "It may be delayed but not denied."

Nehemiah 8:10 says, "Then he said unto them, Go your way, eat the fat, and drink the sweet, and send portions unto them for whom nothing is prepared: for *this* day *is* holy unto our Lord: neither be ye sorry; for the joy of the LORD is your strength." This text comes on the heels of the wall of Jerusalem being repaired from the ravages of war. Ezra reads from the word of God and the people bowed their head in worship to God and said amen. Nehemiah's role in the process was to make sure that the wall got built to stabilize the city. Together, Ezra and Nehemiah made sure that the people understood the word of God and what it meant for them. Verse 10 essentially tells the people to be a blessing to your selves and to others, but on the tail end of the scripture it says, "For the joy of the Lord is our strength." In this scripture we find three important points.

1. Be blessed
2. Be a blessing
3. Recognize the presence of the Lord in our days
4. Bring the Lord joy in those days

Why Praise

When God gets joy out of our lives then the glory of the Lord will fall on us. It is at this point that we feel the presence of the Holy Spirit bringing affirmation to our relationship with Jesus Christ and filling us with the joy that comes from that connection. When Nehemiah says the joy of the Lord is our strength, he is essentially saying making the Lord Glad becomes our refuge or our safe place. Not just one time but a continual refuge from the storms of life. In this place of refuge we are released to be blessed, be a blessing, honor the Lord throughout our day, and bring the Lord more joy because we can't help but tell others how good He is to us. By doing so, verse 15 of John 15 becomes our new title.

❖ [15] Henceforth I call you not servants; for the servant knoweth not what his lord doeth: but I have called you friends; for all things that I have heard of my Father I have made known unto you. [16] Ye have not chosen me, but I have chosen you, and ordained you, that ye should go and bring forth fruit, and *that* your fruit should remain: that whatsoever ye shall ask of the Father in my name, he may give it you.

This is not a presumptuous position but one bestowed upon those who make Christ their lifelong pursuit. We are called to be servants to humanity for the sake of the gospel. But this text is the response of the Savior to those who willingly say yes in service to God the Father. In doing so, we get a name change. Jesus calls us friend. Why praise? We want a name change.

Chapter XI Amazing Grace

"Amazing grace how sweet the sound that saved a wretch like me. I once was lost but now I'm found was blind but now I see." These words have been sung in every way imaginable. But when they are heard from the lips of an ex slave ship owner they take on a different connotation. They seem to ring more profoundly because they come from the heart of a man who knows what it is to feel the weight of sin. Not just the sin within, but sin perpetrated on others by him. In the movie "Amazing Grace" heralding the story of William Wilberforce, John Newton his pastor and the writer of the song, says something I think is simplistically profound. John's memory was fading because of age, so he was in the process of writing his last memoirs. The scene shows Pastor Newton encouraging William to take up his campaign for the abolition of slave trade in Great Britain. John Newton says, "I remember two things quite clearly, I am a great sinner and Christ is a great savior." In order for us to truly appreciate the love of God and the sacrifice of Christ at Calvary, There must be a keen awareness of our condition prior to the love of God. John Newton wrote Amazing Grace because he recognized the leniency of God to allow him to earn his living through the abuse, debasement, and affliction of African people. The condition of their lives and God's mercy in his life had affected him, so that he wrote

Why Praise

Amazing Grace. Hundreds of thousands of people of every color, nationality, and creed have sung that song born out of a liberated soul in hopes of being liberated themselves. Little did John Newton realize he was not just writing a song for himself, but for all who would need a way to express amazing grace. Our understanding of God's love hinges on our perception of grace. But our perception of grace is connected to our conviction over our sin. Luke chapter 7 beginning with verse 36 tells of an interesting account concerning Jesus and a sinner woman.

> ❖ ³⁶ And one of the Pharisees desired him that he would eat with him. And he went into the Pharisee's house, and sat down to meat. ³⁷ And, behold, a woman in the city, which was a sinner, when she knew that *Jesus* sat at meat in the Pharisee's house, brought an alabaster box of ointment, ³⁸ And stood at his feet behind *him* weeping, and began to wash his feet with tears, and did wipe *them* with the hairs of her head, and kissed his feet, and anointed *them* with the ointment. ³⁹ Now when the Pharisee which had bidden him saw *it*, he spake within himself, saying, This man, if he were a prophet, would have known who and what manner of woman *this is* that toucheth him: for she is a sinner. ⁴⁰ And Jesus answering said unto him, Simon, I have somewhat to say unto thee. And he saith, Master, say on. ⁴¹ There was a certain creditor which had two debtors: the one owed five hundred pence, and the other fifty. ⁴² And when they had nothing to pay, he frankly forgave them both. Tell me therefore, which of them will love him most? ⁴³ Simon answered and said, I suppose that *he*, to whom he forgave most. And he said unto him, Thou hast rightly judged. ⁴⁴ And he turned to the woman, and said unto Simon, Seest thou this woman? I entered into thine house,

thou gavest me no water for my feet: but she hath washed my feet with tears, and wiped *them* with the hairs of her head. [45] Thou gavest me no kiss: but this woman since the time I came in hath not ceased to kiss my feet. [46] My head with oil thou didst not anoint: but this woman hath anointed my feet with ointment. [47] Wherefore I say unto thee, Her sins, which are many, are forgiven; for she loved much: but to whom little is forgiven, *the same* loveth little. [48] And he said unto her, Thy sins are forgiven. [49] And they that sat at meat with him began to say within themselves, Who is this that forgiveth sins also? [50] And he said to the woman, Thy faith hath saved thee; go in peace.

Jesus is invited to a Pharisees house for a meal. Jesus accepts. Evidently news travels fast, because just as they sat down to eat, a woman of the village comes in with an expensive bottle of perfume. Knowing who Jesus was she begins her own ritual of purification. She stands at His feet weeping. Her tears are a sign of an inward conviction over her own sinful condition. So she does the only thing she knows how to do, serve. She is use to service because she makes her living as the town harlot. Her life is filled with the request of men to meet their needs. At every level she is a servant. So, there is no strain in her to serve the Lord, but this time her service is not only about the service but purification and worship. This woman is working something out of herself that has work itself in her over a lifetime. As she cries, she lets down her hair, dries Jesus' feet with her hair, proceeds to kiss His feet and then takes an alabaster box of ointment and anoints his feet. As I read the story, I can feel the utter conviction of her lifestyle provoking her to this response. It is as if she has no other course of action but to let her gift of service bless Jesus. I would imagine that she had some money or something else of value but it was not

Why Praise

enough. What she was good at and most comfortable with was her service. So she used what she had trusting that Jesus would know her heart. The people around her saw her for what she was but she hoped Jesus would she her for what she wanted to be. She was a great sinner in need of great Savior. The people began to whisper about her reputation and Jesus' supposed prophet status, but Jesus knowing the inclination of their hearts addressed Simon and by overhearing the onlookers would be dealt with as well. He tells a parable of a creditor who forgives two debtors. One owed a little and the other a lot. Jesus asked Simon which one would appreciate forgiveness the most, the one forgiven a little or the one forgiven a lot and Simon says the one that was forgiven a lot. Jesus says you are right. At this point Jesus makes some stark comparisons on relationship and hospitality. Jesus says to Simon.

1. I entered your house you gave me no water for my feet	1. She washed my feet with her tears and wiped them with her hair
2. Gave me no Kiss	2. Since I came in she has not ceased to kiss my feet
3. You did not anoint my head with oil	3. She anointed my feet with ointment or perfume

The implication of the event is found in verse 47. Wherefore I say unto thee, Her sins, which are many, are forgiven; for she loved much: but to whom little is forgiven, *the same* loveth little. Her life was filled with loving moments but they were also connected to a sinful lifestyle. She understood the implication of sin and its' affects on a life because it was her livelihood. Because she lived a life of sin and was acutely aware of her need for deliverance, grace and forgiveness were not just words but an act of absolution. They were her freedom papers. In other words, being

Why Praise

forgiven would give her a new lease on life a new name from which to operate. Simon on the other hand as well as the onlookers, because of their place in culture took grace and forgiveness for granted because in their mind they had not really done anything that bad. They were good people rather than being sinful creatures. Our appreciation of God's grace and love is weakened or strengthened by our perception of our selves. Whether we are good or bad, while this is important, is really incidental. If we think more of ourselves than we ought then what Christ did at Calvary becomes a historical account rather than a loving act from a loving God on behalf of a sinful creature. We are sinners saved by grace but there is also a need to remember why Gods love is so precious. We once were lost but now were found were blind but not we see. We are no longer numbered with the transgressors but with the children of God heirs and joint-heirs with Christ. Our name change entitles us to relationship that leans on God's qualification of who we are. Once we accept Jesus Christ as our personal Savior we are no longer a sinner but a saint. We may sin because of our connection to this world but we do not dwell there because we are not of this world. Jesus paid it all. Our debt is paid in full and we are the righteous family of God. And because we are attached to Jesus the Christ by blood we can ask what we will so that it will glorify our Father. John 14:13-14, John 15:7-8, John 16:23-24, all make reference to us asking what we will and God giving it. In a world where sickness and disease run rampant, violence, negligence, and abuse are main stays why won't God answer. We know people are praying and hoping, but still no change. I submit to you that the children have not cried. 2 Chronicles 7:13-14 say's:

> ❖ [13] If I shut up heaven that there be no rain, or if I command the locusts to devour the land, or if I send pestilence among my people; [14] If my people, which

are called by my name, shall humble themselves, and pray, and seek my face, and turn from their wicked ways; then will I hear from heaven, and will forgive their sin, and will heal their land.

We the children of God are called out of darkness into the marvelous light. We are the remnant of God in the earth. We are the salt and light. We are the blood bought fire baptized believers in the Most High God. We are the children of God. This passage of scripture comes out of Solomon finishing the house of God. The people have feasted and have been sent home happy. The Lord appears to Solomon by night and gives Him a powerful and prophetic word. Notice verse 13, If I shut up heaven that there be no rain, or if I command the locusts to devour the land, or if I send pestilence among my people. This scripture essentially states that God will allow certain things to happen to us and our world. Our response to that as human beings is if God loves us so much why won't God protect us from such horrors. First of all, there are many things that could have happened to us but God blocked it. Secondly, we live in a world filled with evil intentions a part from the goodness of God. But even though God allows such terrible things to persist, He gave us an antidote. According to Heb 13:8, Jesus is the same yesterday today and forever. Jesus being the expressed image of God in the flesh we can surmise God to also be the same yesterday, today and forever. This being true verse 14 is the remedy for much of our dilemma. As children of God and called by God we have the power to affect change in the heart of God so that it blesses our world. If my people, which are called by my name, shall humble themselves, and pray, and seek my face, and turn from their wicked ways; then will I hear from heaven, and will forgive their sin, and will heal their land. The answer to what is wrong with us as a world is in our relationship to God. There will always be some sort of issue attacking humanity, but the relationship we have with God has overcome the world even our faith. But as long as we struggle as believers with who we are, what we are, and why we are here problems will continue to persist simply because we do not know where to throw the praise. The premier desire of God is that no one be lost. We have been made friends of God to help in that pursuit. We are not here to judge or condemn. Matt 5:9 says, "Blessed are the peacemakers for they shall be called the children of God." We are here to show the love of Christ in and for the world so that no one misses the great home going celebration. The whole reason why God loves us is so that we can have the assurance there is more to life than what we see. God extended His love towards us in that while we were yet sinners Christ died. Who we are in God is not something that we deserve but something that is bestowed. This is the love of God manifested. Jesus was so committed to God the Father that He was willing to sacrifice His life so that we could have relationship and live. He and the Father were all right but we and the Father were not. So, out of His love for God Jesus says I'll humble myself and die. Jesus bridged the gap between us and God. Now, all we have to do now is cry Abba Father and the relationship will speak for itself. Why Praise you ask? So the relationship can speak. Our praise is not just noise, but an affirmation to the economy of God for our condition as a fallen creation.

We were afflicted with a terrible condition called sin. It affected our love and our life. But if we love God and respond to that love with devotion and dedication, we can ask what we will and it shall be done. Herein is the Father glorified!

John 17
❖ ^{1} These words spake Jesus, and lifted up his eyes to heaven, and said, Father, the hour is come; glorify thy Son, that thy Son also may glorify thee: ^{2} As thou

Why Praise

hast given him power over all flesh, that he should give eternal life to as many as thou hast given him. [3] And this is life eternal, that they might know thee the only true God, and Jesus Christ, whom thou hast sent. [4] I have glorified thee on the earth: I have finished the work which thou gavest me to do. [5] And now, O Father, glorify thou me with thine own self with the glory which I had with thee before the world was.

❖ [18] As thou hast sent me into the world, even so have I also sent them into the world

Let your light so shine before men that they may see your good works and glorify the Father which is in Heaven.

Printed in the United States
136441LV00001B/8/P